Whitechapel in the 1880s, from a contemporary map. The sites showing are marked

1: [Bucks Row, n]ow Durward Street) where the body of Mary Nicholls was found on August 31

2: 29 Hanbury Street, where Annie Chapman was found on September 8

3: Berners Street, where Elizabeth Stride was found on September 30

4: Mitre Square, where Catherine Eddowes was found on September 30

5: Miller's Court, an alley off Dorset Street, where Mary Kelly was found on November 9

6: 140 The Minories, Dr Lionel Druitt's surgery

H: The London Hospital

Gordon Cobban.
Christmas 1972.

JACK THE RIPPER

Jack the Ripper

DANIEL FARSON

LONDON

MICHAEL JOSEPH

First published in Great Britain by Michael Joseph Ltd
52 Bedford Square, London, W.C.1
1972

7181 1050 1

Set and printed in Great Britain
by Tonbridge Printers Ltd, Tonbridge, Kent
in Plantin ten on twelve point,
on paper supplied by P. F. Bingham Ltd,
and bound by James Burn at Esher, Surrey

Contents

CONTENTS

THREE: THE ANSWER

Illustrations

Acknowledgements

Grateful acknowledgement is made of permission to quote from *Jack the Ripper* by Robin Odell, published by George G. Harrap & Co. Ltd., and from *The Mystery of Jack the Ripper* by Leonard Matters, published by W. H. Allen & Co. Ltd. Illustrations nos. 1, 3, 4, 5, 6, 7 and 12 are reproduced by kind permission of the Commissioner of City Police; and the photograph of M. J. Druitt by kind permission of the Warden and Fellows of Winchester College. Illustration no. 15 is from the Radio Times Hulton Picture Library.

Foreword by Professor Francis Camps

Criminological problems have always exercised peculiar fascination for members of the public, especially when connected with murder. When such murders occurred many years ago and the information concerning them is limited in character, then they present great scope for speculation and publication. Unfortunately, little such speculation sheds light on the original problem, partly because of lack of research and partly because the authors, frequently, have made up their minds beforehand and have built the story up to fit in with their own ideas. When, as in the case of Jack the Ripper, the sensational involvement of a member of the Royal Family, who cannot reply, appears, you come to a state of pure chaos.

I was interested in Jack the Ripper long before the 'Royal' theory was put forward and avidly seized on by the press. I would say unhesitatingly that I reject it not only as incorrect but also as a great intrusion on privacy for the purpose of publicity. This suggestion had, in fact, been made to me several years earlier by one of the really great authorities on the subject of Jack the Ripper. I rejected it then.

My own interest in Jack the Ripper arose from my association with the London Hospital, near which nearly all the murders occurred. The hospital was also connected with the theory that a surgeon was responsible for the murders, because he was either revenging his son who had caught venereal disease, or looking for the person who had infected him. This seemed plausible because of the erroneous idea that only a surgeon could have caused the mutilation or found the organs which were removed. In fact, there was a genuine connection with the London Hospital insomuch as the Curator of the Museum received a kidney which almost certainly was removed from one of the bodies. This did not mean that the murderer was necessarily part of the hospital.

From a criminological point of view there are certain questions and features about the murders which have to be explained in order to arrive at some idea of the identity of the perpetrator. First of all, they took place at regular intervals during a limited period. Then, they increased in the degree of mutilation, each one being worse than the last, culminating with the final one, clearly the first in which the murderer had unlimited time. Then again, murders of this type only stop when the murderer is either dead or incarcerated; we must ask, why did 'The Ripper' disappear so quickly from the scene of the crime?

None of the number of theories put forward in the past have satisfactorily dealt with these problems. The reason for this is that everybody has been thrashing around for some sort of explanation. I have already mentioned the 'surgeon theory' and the 'member of the Royal Family theory', both of which I think must be discarded. The knowledge of how to remove organs is not limited to the medical profession. Studying the valuable information shown by the pictures which were discovered in the basement of the London Hospital and which is confirmed by pictures in the City of London police museum, one realises that far from being the work of skilled surgeon, any surgeon who operated in this manner would have been struck off the Medical Register. One should then consider other people who might have surgical knowledge but be, as it were, in the early stages of medical knowledge, and might have given the perpetrator the opportunity of access to books.

Farson has, I think, provided for the first time an explanation which will really fit in with the true facts. It is his research which has revealed this, a research uncovering information which was not generally known before. If the culprit he suggests satisfy three criteria – have been associated with the medical profession, have had access to somewhere in the neighbourhood where he could disappear at short notice, and finally have died within a reasonably short time of the last murder – I feel that we are getting very near the truth.

The so-called 'Nude Murders' not long ago in London, while not involving mutilation, bore a close resemblance to those of the Ripper. When the police eventually discovered the murderer – (in their view), it was shown that this person had in fact died soon after the last murder.

This is true of Farson's suspect too. It does a great deal of credit to Farson that he has followed this up, though I am not saying that other people have not done so in the past. Colin Wilson, who to the best of my knowledge knows more about this subject than anybody, would enter into it in great detail, but I think most writers miss this very small point which matters crucially.

To
Colin Wilson
the most generous
of friends
and authors
and to the
memory of
Francis Camps

Introduction

Nearly a hundred years after the events the name of Jack the Ripper provokes the imagination like no other criminal, not even Christie or the Boston Strangler. New Scotland Yard receives an average of three letters a day about Jack the Ripper. East End tours lead visitors around the sites of the murders. The British seem obsessed. He has been 'celebrated' in novels like *The Lodger* by Mrs Belloc Lowndes and in countless films: the first was directed by Alfred Hitchcock and rather surprisingly the lead was played by Ivor Novello. The latest film version was *The Hands of the Ripper,* released by Hammer. Many books have been written about the Ripper and continue to be written. Probably no other crime has attracted so many amateur criminologists with unlikely if colourful theories of their own. As recently as 1970 it was seriously suggested that the Ripper was the Duke of Clarence, heir to the English throne. This libellous but entertaining story received a great deal of publicity and I doubt if we have heard the last of it. Even now, it would not surprise me if people came forward with sensational 'new evidence'. Far from shame attaching to any association with the murderer, there is eagerness to claim relationship. Some people are so possessive that they have written me indignant letters saying that the Ripper was undoubtedly their own relative. There have been confessions. I am only surprised that there hasn't been a 'Ripper Claimant', but maybe there is still time for a son or grandson to stake the claim on his behalf.

Through the inspiration of Colin Wilson I became myself an amateur criminologist and in 1959 I became part of the story. This happened by accident. I was staying with Lady Rose McLaren in North Wales and mentioned the television programmes I was preparing on the Ripper.

'That's an extraordinary coincidence,' she said, and explained that we were going to visit her mother-in-law, the Dowager Lady Aberconway, that same afternoon. A few hours later at Maenan Hall, I explained my interest to Christabel Aberconway and she was kind enough to give me her father's private notes which she had copied out soon after his death. At the time I hardly realised the discovery that lay in my hands, for her father, Sir Melville Macnaghten, had been in charge of the CID after the last Ripper murder and it had been his task to complete the file on the murderer. Because the official Scotland Yard files will not be open to the public until 1992, no one has known the name of the man whom the police suspected. Now, for the first time, this name lay in my hands.

I finished my television programmes. At Lady Aberconway's request I gave the suspect's initials only: M.J.D. Since then my discovery has been the basis for various investigations and publications and the full name has been revealed. While these other publications confirm the original facts they have not taken them further. Indeed they stop at the very point where it *is* possible to take them further. This is why I decided to continue and complete my own research and unearth enough new evidence about the suspect to close the file, once and for all, on the compelling mystery of Jack the Ripper.

One : The Murders

i: *The Setting*

Not only London but all England experienced a surge of panic in 1888. This contrasts with the comparative lack of public interest in the Nude Murders of 1964 when six prostitutes were found choked and stripped in London alleyways and beside the Thames. The murderer was never caught, but the police suspected a security guard who had gassed himself after the last murder. These murders had such a remarkable parallel to the Whitechapel murders that the police referred to 'Jack the Stripper'.

Why did the Ripper cause such panic? Why such terror when the act of murder was commonplace? Partly because it *was* commonplace. In 1888 the East End was a sprawling port, a melting pot of nationalities, an overcrowded, festering wound, a cesspool of violence, poverty and prostitution. Murder was so frequent that when two neighbours heard a cry of 'murder!' early in the morning as the last victim was being killed, they ignored it.

The Ripper was the climax, the breaking point. The conscience of the nation was shocked. Panic was waiting to be kindled and the Ripper was the torch. Terror spread because of the Ripper's skill. He struck swiftly at week-ends over a period of only six weeks. He worked in the small area of Spitalfields and Whitechapel. With the final exception of Mary Kelly, the victims were middle-aged prostitutes and had their throats cut in public throughfares. All save one were mutilated and her body was spared only because the murderer was interrupted. The rumours surrounding the mutilations heightened the panic. What mutilations? What parts were taken from the bodies? Surely not those parts that most newspapers dared not mention by name? Then there was the manner in which the

19

Ripper escaped within seconds, inevitably spattered with blood, still clutching the tools of his trade, disappearing as if by some black magic.

Finally there was that name, with which he – or someone else – signed the letters to the agencies. The name of 'Jack the Ripper' – fearfully accurate – was the fiendish finishing touch. No wonder that for years afterwards East Enders used his name to threaten their children when they misbehaved.

The murderer's chosen area, too, was as conducive to this terror as it was to the easy commission of his crimes. Seldom can a murderer have found such an easy pitch. The East End was the final refuge of the derelict. Already there was a sort of anarchy. Large numbers of German, Russian and Polish Jews were unable to speak or read English. There was a constant flow of foreign seamen who stepped ashore eager for drink and sex and were quickly robbed. As Leonard Matters wrote 'the contrast between the East End and the West End is the contrast between poverty, squalor and degradation, and wealth, comfort and luxury, flaunted by the few in the face of the many'. He wrote this in 1928; thirty years later when I moved into the district I could still find the traces. In particular I remember the methylated-spirit drinkers sitting among the shattered gravestones beside Whitechapel Road, and faces in Brick Street with staring black eyes.

In 1888 Whitechapel and Spitalfields were so overcrowded that it was common for small houses to have as many as twenty-four people sharing them. People rented a bed for fourpence and slept in shifts. It was estimated that fifteen thousand men, women and children were homeless, and 128,000 were cared for by work-houses. The streets at night were full of people, and though pubs were closed officially at one in the morning, many stayed open through the night.

Prostitution was an accepted fact of life throughout London – the Bishop of Exeter claimed there were 80,000 prostitutes there altogether – and the most wretched and unsuccessful of the women ended up in the East End. It does not necessarily follow that the Ripper had a grudge against prostitutes in particular: they were the easiest prey. They roamed the shadows searching for customers and only when their luck seemed hopeless did they seek the protection of a doss-house. There was little encouragement to do this for the conditions inside such places were abject.

In his inquest on one of the victims the Coroner, Wynne Baxter, referred to the manner in which the women were herded like cattle: 'The glimpses of life in those dens which the evidence in this case discloses is sufficient to make us feel that there is much in nineteenth-century civilisation of which we have small reason to be proud; but you, who are constantly called together to hear the sad tale of starvation, or semi-starvation, of misery, immorality and wickedness, which some of the occupants of the 5,000 beds in this district have every week to relate at coroners' inquests, do not require to be reminded of what life in a Spitalfields lodging-house means.'

Admission to these doss-houses cost fourpence, but sometimes the victim did not even have that.

Many people imagine that the Ripper murdered a large number of women over a long period of time. This is not true. His moment was short and swift. Several women before, and many afterwards, were attributed to the Ripper but it was accepted by the police that 'the Whitechapel murderer had five victims and five only'.

Two earlier victims often suggested are Emma Smith and Martha Turner.

Emma Elizabeth Smith was a 'drunken Whitechapel prostitute', but there are few other resemblances between the later Ripper murders and this victim. Emma Smith, aged forty-five, was attacked when staggering home to her lodgings in Spitalfields about four in the morning on Tuesday 3 April 1888, the night after the revels of Easter Monday. Before she died in hospital twenty-four hours later she was able to tell the police that she had been attacked by four men, the youngest around nineteen years old. She had been stabbed by a sharp instrument like a spike. Her few coins were taken and this seems an ordinary case of robbery by one of the gangs – like the notorious Nichol Gang – which attacked prostitutes. Writing eleven years later, Walter Besant said that 'hustling the people in the street is natural. The boys gather together and hold the street; if anyone ventures to pass through it they rush upon him, knock him down, and kick him savagely about the head; they rob him as well. In the autumn of last year [1899] an inoffensive elderly gentleman was knocked down by such a gang, robbed, kicked about the head, and taken up insensible; he was carried home and died the next day.'

If Emma Smith's murder had not been followed quickly by two more, all within 300 yards of each other, her name would be forgotten.

Martha Turner (or Tabram) is the second supposed victim, and is of far greater interest. This murder also took place in the early hours following a Bank Holiday and Martha Turner was also a prostitute. She was thirty-five but a photograph suggests she looked considerably older. It would seem that the age of these East End prostitutes matched the poverty of their clients. She was married to Hendrik Tabram.

On the evening of Bank Holiday Monday, a young soldier was seen drinking at the Two Brewers, one of the many riverside pubs at Limehouse. Later he was seen with Martha Turner in another pub, the Angel and Crown, drinking with two friends: another soldier and another prostitute. Martha's body was found on Tuesday 7 August on the first landing of George Yard Buildings in Commercial Street. A married couple climbed these stairs at two o'clock and saw nothing. At three-thirty a cab driver called Albert Crow noticed a body lying there but as this was quite usual he passed on. It was only in the early light of five o'clock that another lodger leaving for work saw the body was that of a woman lying on her back in a pool of blood, and called the police. The doctor was startled to find as many as thirty-nine stab wounds – nine in the throat, seventeen in the breast, thirteen in the stomach. But her throat was not cut and there was no mutilation. It seemed as if the stabbing had been done in a frenzy with two weapons at once, which started the rumour that the murderer was ambidextrous. One of the weapons was thought to be a bayonet and all the soldiers of the Tower were lined up for an identity parade, including the two young soldiers who had been seen with Turner in the pub and had been arrested. The other prostitute 'failed or rather *refused* to identify' the murderer, wrote Macnaghten in his private notes. Plainly, Macnaghten suspected the first soldier. But the first murder that Macnaghten accepted as the work of the Ripper took place twenty-four days later, that of Mary Nichols.

ii: *The First Killings*

Mary Ann Nicholls (or Nichols) was a pathetic creature, down on her luck if anyone was. She was married with five children but her husband had left her. She worked as a domestic help until she stole £3 for drink and was sacked. She had struggled along as a prostitute for the previous few months, with a desolate doss-house in Spitalfields as her home – until eventually even this place rejected her. She was indeed 'an unfortunate' as the Victorians described a prostitute. Forty-two years old, short and sallow with five front teeth missing, she cannot have had much success in her profession, for she was unable to raise the four pennies demanded by the doss-house for her bed on the night of 31 August.

But she had spirit. As she was turned away, she boasted that she'd soon earn her money and be back: 'Look what a jolly bonnet I've got,' she cried. Either she hoped to sell it, or tempt some admirer – probably the latter, for the bonnet was found later beside her body. Somehow she did raise a few pennies, but she spent it all on drink. When she was seen for the last time, by her friend 'Nelly' Holland, she was almost helpless: ' "Polly" Nicholls was very drunk and staggered

23

against the wall.' Certainly she was in no state to fight for her
life as she fled, or was taken by her murderer, to the comparative quiet of Bucks Row. It seems as if the murderer put
a hand over her mouth and cut her throat from behind. No
cry, no sound was heard by a woman wide awake only a few
yards away in one of the houses.

Her body was found at the entrance to an old stableyard by
a carter called Cross, who thought the bundle might be a
useful tarpaulin, and another workman. When they saw the
blood they ran for a policeman and while they were reporting
the murder another constable also found the body having passed
the same spot only half an hour earlier. The time was approximately 3:45 a.m. Neither he, nor anyone else, had seen or
heard anything suspicious.

Incredibly, the extent of the injuries were not realised, though
her intestines protruded from the body. They were not noticed
by the local doctor. Dr Ralph Llewellyn, who was annoyed
at being woken and barely made an examination before order-
ing the body to be taken to the mortuary at the Old Montague
Street Workhouse. It was here that the attendant, one of the
workhouse paupers, lifted up her clothes and was sick when he
discovered that 'she had been disembowelled' (*The Times*).
The whole affair was bungled because the man then stripped
and washed the body down, possibly removing important
evidence.

The *Star* was sufficiently shocked to describe the injuries in
detail:

> The throat is cut in two gashes, the instrument having been
> a sharp one, but used in a ferocious and reckless way. There
> is a gash under the left ear, reaching nearly to the centre of
> the throat. Along half its length, however, it is accompanied
> by another one which reaches around under the other ear,
> making a wide and horrible hole, and nearly severing the
> head from the body. The ghastliness of this cut, however,
> pales into insignificance alongside the other. No murder was
> ever more ferociously and more brutally done. The knife,

which must have been a large and sharp one, was jabbed into the deceased at the lower part of the abdomen, and then drawn upwards, not once but twice. The first cut veered to the right, slitting up the groin, and passing over the left hip, but the second cut went straight upward, along the centre of the body, and reaching to the breast-bone. Such horrible work could only be the deed of a maniac.

The ferocity this conveys – the knife drawn *upwards* not once but twice – was evidenced in the later murders and explains why people could look at the bodies and tell at a glance that this was the work of one man, and one man only.

Of all the murder sites, Bucks Row remains much the same today. The same cobbled stones and yard entrance are there, though the slaughter-house, which made neighbouring butchers and slaughtermen suspect at the time, has gone. But the name has changed: the residents were ashamed of their sudden notoriety and outraged by a postman who took a macabre delight in knocking at their doors asking 'Number 5 Killer Row I believe?' As a result of a petition, Bucks Row became 'Durward Street' as it is today, a few yards from the roar of Whitechapel Road. It is about to be demolished.

In 1959 a ninety-year-old man, Mr Wright, who lived in Bucks Row when he was a boy, showed me the spot where the murder took place – or at least where the body was found. His father was a carter at the stable-yard who got up to feed the horses at five o'clock in the morning. A crowd had arrived from the factory opposite and he ordered his son to wash down some congealed blood. But police officers reported that surprisingly little blood had been found; it was even suspected, for a moment, that the body had been moved.

The first note of panic had been struck. The murder immediately attracted attention because of the similarity with the murders of Emma Smith and Martha Turner. *The Times* concluded: 'All three were of the class called unfortunates. The three murders were committed within three hundred yards of each other. Police believe that this is the work of one individual.' (This last statement conflicts with Macnaghten's notes, but perhaps the police did believe this at the time.)

The rumours and witch-hunts began. It was said that Mary Nicholls had been friendly with a man known as 'Leather Apron' and immediately anyone faintly answering such a description was suspect, shoe-makers in particular. A Mr Anderson has told me: 'I was a child then and well remember the sensation. We'd pick on some harmless old man and as many as fifty kids would pursue him shouting "Jack the Ripper" [this dates the incident as some time later]. We also called people "Leather Apron", and the local sweetshop started to make a new toffee called "Leather Apron Toffee".'

But for the people affected, the Leather Apron scare was far from amusing. A Polish Jew called John Pizer was arrested at his house in Whitechapel and charged with the murder. This sparked off a surge of anti-semitism and when Pizer was publicly cleared by the Coroner at the inquest he was held for another twenty-four hours, probably to escape mob violence. He had the courage to sue, and sue successfully, the newspapers who had rashly identified him as the murderer.

At the inquest there was the first hint of 'medical knowledge'. The doctor suggested that the murderer was left-handed and said the mutilations were 'deftly and fairly skilfully performed'. Nicholls's father testified that she was a 'a dissolute character and a drunkard whom he knew would come to a bad end'. But her husband had more charity; as he identified the body he said sadly, 'I forgive you for what you did to me, now that I find you like this.'

Only eight days later the Ripper struck again. The victim was Annie Chapman, sometimes known as 'Dark Annie', another pathetic old prostitute – at least old for those days in that district. She was forty-seven, looked fifty-five and was dying of consumption. Like so many of her colleagues she had known better days and like Mary Nicholls she was turned out of her doss-house in Dorset Street at two in the morning because she lacked the few pennies for her bed. 'No money, no bed,' the keeper told her. She gave the weary reply: 'I have not got it. I am weak and ill and have been in the infirmary.'

Her body was found at six in the morning in the backyard of 29 Hanbury Street by John Davis, a porter, who lived on the top floor with his wife. Sixteen people shared the house and the front room was lived in by a Mrs Hardman and her son who also used it as a shop to sell cats' meat. The front door was never locked; it led to a passage which was twenty-five feet long. This gave access to the stairs and at the end of the passage was the small yard frequently used by drunks and prostitutes in the night.

I met a charming old man who, as a boy at the time, was driving through Hanbury Street at dawn, perched on the back of a cart. Hearing the cry of 'Murder!' his curiosity got the better of him and he jumped off to find out what had happened, losing his job in consequence.

'There she was,' he told me in a soft and gentle voice. 'All her entrails steamin' 'ot. And I'll never forget it because she had red-and-white stockings on.'

News of the murder spread rapidly, with the realisation that the two murders of Nicholls and Chapman – were only a few hundred yards apart and almost certainly by the same hand. Neighbours charged a small fee for a view of the murder site, and one woman claimed she had seen a message scrawled on the door of No. 29: 'This is the fourth. I will murder sixteen more and then give myself up.'

The details concerning the corpse were even more terrible this time, though once again the body had been washed down before a proper examination could be made and the conditions of the mortuary were exposed as deplorable. The Coroner, at the inquest held in the Working Lads' Institute, Whitechapel Road, complained that there was no authorised mortuary for the district, which 'made it almost impossible for a proper post-mortem examination to be carried out'.

He also made the remarkable claim, 'Undoubtedly Nicholls and Chapman were murdered for some object, to secure some pathological specimen from the abdomen.'

Annie Chapman's head had been nearly severed from her

body and a handkerchief wrapped around her neck as if to hold it together. The face was bruised and the tongue swollen as if the Ripper had clasped her from behind and pressed his hand over her mouth to prevent her from screaming. Again the body had been disembowelled and this time the womb had been removed. Dr Bagster Phillips claimed that the removal of a kidney and the ovaries showed great anatomical knowledge, but he was reluctant to go into further details which 'could only be painful to the feelings of the jury and public'. When pressed to do so by the Coroner, the court was cleared of women and boys and he gave evidence which *The Times* described as 'totally unfit for publication'.

However, the *Lancet* reported it in grisly but revealing detail: 'The abdomen had been entirely laid open; the intestines, severed from their mesenteric attachments, had been lifted out of the body, and placed on the shoulder of the corpse; whilst from the pelvis the uterus and its appendages with the upper portion of the vagina and the posterior two-thirds of the bladder, had been entirely removed. No trace of these parts could be found ... Obviously the work was that of an expert – of one, at least, who had such knowledge of anatomical or pathological examinations as to be enabled to secure the pelvic organs with one sweep of the knife, which must therefore ... have been at least five inches long ...' It was suggested that the sweep went from left to right. The Coroner concluded, 'No unskilled person could have done this. It must have been someone used to the post-mortem room. The conclusion that the desire was to possess the missing abdominal organ seems overwhelming.' I shall suggest later that he over-stressed the point about medical knowledge.

The removal of the womb has led Colin Wilson, in *A Casebook of Murder*, to draw this conclusion:

The Ripper was not interested in the genitals; his fantasies were all about cutting bellies. It was the womb itself that fascinated him. Freudians will draw a great many inferences from this – about hatred of the mother, perhaps of younger

28

brothers and sisters stealing the parents' affection, etc. I would draw only one inference: that this destruction of the womb indicated a suicidal tendency in the Ripper; it was the place that bore him about which he felt ambivalent.

This has direct relevance to my own investigations for I shall show that Jack the Ripper did indeed commit suicide and almost certainly did have an obsession about his mother.

The police were desperate for evidence and clues: those they found were curious and unhelpful. In a corner of the yard there was part of a bloodstained envelope with the crest of the Sussex Regiment and under the tap was a leather apron. Even more bewildering was a curious detail that seems inexplicable, though I cannot help feeling that it has significance: two brass rings, two new farthings, and a few coins were laid out neatly around the feet of the corpse.

Although Dr Bagster Phillips explained some of the cruder slashes as due to speed, the Ripper seems to have taken his time over this particular murder. Then once again he disappeared, walking through streets when there must have been a number of workers on their way to the markets. Chief Inspector Abberline drew the obvious conclusion – that the Ripper knew the district and its maze of passages very well indeed. This point is undeniable. *The Times* wondered how the murderer could have left Hanbury Street 'reeking with blood, and yet . . . he must have walked in broad daylight along streets comparatively well frequented, even at that early hour, without his startling appearance attracting the slightest attention'.

For some reason it was assumed that the murderer must be a member of the 'lower' classes. Queen Victoria could hardly bring herself to believe the murderer was an Englishman; it was impossible that he might be a gentleman. Consequently the doss-houses were searched and watched, though they were the one place where the murderer would have been spotted instantly. *The Times* drew a more sensible conclusion: 'He is a man lodging in a comparatively decent house in the district, to which he would be able to retire quickly, and in which, once it was reached, he would be able at his leisure to remove from his person all traces of his hideous crime.' That too is a vital point to remember, confirmed by the deduction of Forbes-Winslow. A specialist in mental diseases, he wrote to *The Times* that he felt sure that 'the murderer was to be found in the "upper classes of society" '.

On 9 September, the day after the murder, twelve people were taken to Commercial Street Police Station, the first of many false alarms and false arrests. When Pizer, the 'Leather Apron' suspect, was present at the inquest on Annie Chapman it was explained that it was necessary to bring the man forward for his own protection. When asked why he had stayed indoors for several days in succession, he answered, 'Because of the false suspicions against me. If I had gone out and had been found in the streets after this last murder I should have been torn to pieces.'

Another suspect, observed in Gravesend with fresh blood on his clothes and hands, was taken to Commercial Street Police Station by Inspector Abberline. William Piggott gave the explanation that he had seen a woman fall down in Brick Lane at 4:30 in the morning but when he went to pick her up she bit his hand. Women failed to pick him out at an identity parade and he was released, only to be committed to an asylum.

Inspector Abberline had more reason in suspecting a porter from Spitalfields Market called John Richardson, whose mother lived at 29 Hanbury Street. 'I am greatly shocked by the murder,' she had declared, 'for my rooms are regularly used for prayer meetings and both me and my landlord are very angry that a slur should have been put on the respectability of the house.' Now she faced the further distress of finding her own son suspected of the murder. He admitted he had gone to the house just before five o'clock that morning, to see if his mother was all right, but had noticed nothing unusual when he looked into the back yard. He admitted that the leather apron under the tap belonged to him, and also that he had stopped at the entrance to the yard to trim some loose leather from one of his boots with a knife. He was cleared after both the police and the doctor were satisfied that the knife could not have been the murder weapon. Presumably his own knife was far too short.

It was understandable that the police should thrash about like this, with so little to go on. It was inevitable that the public should demand to know what was being done. Two officials in particular were blamed: Henry Mathews, the Home Secretary, 'helpless, heedless, useless Mr Mathews' as the *Daily Telegraph* described him; and Sir Charles Warren, the unlucky Commissioner of the Metropolitan Police. Warren was an obvious target: a none-too-modern-Major-General with a twirly moustache and monocle, and a reputation for drilling his men to hound the unemployed. 'The whole East End is under a Red Terror. If sheer fright grows into crazed fury,' warned one newspaper, 'we shall hold Mr Mathews and Sir Charles Warren responsible.'

Sir Charles brought touches of grotesque if unintentional humour to relieve the grim reality. Finally, he came up with the suggestion of bloodhounds to track the killer down the alleys of the East End. 'It should have been obvious,' wrote Sir Melville Macnaghten scathingly, after the event, 'that bloodhounds were useless in Whitechapel. I cannot conceive a more impossible locality in which to expect hounds to work, or how any sane individual could ever have dreamt of success in this direction.' Sir Charles volunteered to act as a decoy when two champion hounds – Barnaby and Burgho were brought for training to Hyde Park on 9 October. Every time, the dogs hunted down complete strangers; this was blamed on bad weather conditions. Warren persevered, but worse humiliation followed when the dogs were released for a further trial on Tooting Common and ran away. Telegrams had to be sent to all local police stations to look out for them. Londoners roared with laughter at the fiasco, but their ridicule was coloured with contempt: 'It was incurred too at a time,' wrote Sir Melville Macnaghten, 'when "the man in blue" stood none too high in the public estimation.' In the absence of evidence, both police and public reacted randomly. One scare was that of 'the Man with the Black Bag' when the public seized on the rumour that the murderer carried his tools in a black bag, and chased perfectly innocent bag-owners until they were rescued by the police. Consequently, this useful type of canvas bag went out of fashion.

As the police seemed incompetent, and the government refused to offer any reward, people were tempted to take the law into their own hands. East End tradesmen, a local MP, and even policemen from the Whitechapel Division, raised money to offer a reward of their own. But the lack of a similar reward from the government was resented, and emphasised the fact that to many people the East End might have been a foreign country. Wynne Baxter, the outspoken Coroner, said, 'There can be no question that had these unfortunate women been murdered with equal secrecy in the West End, rewards would not have been withheld.'

The *Star* suggested that the public should protect themselves:

We can talk of larger reforms when we do away with the centralised non-efficient military system which Sir Charles Warren has brought to perfection. The people of the East End must become their own police. They must form themselves at once into vigilance committees. There should be a central committee which should map out the neighbourhood into districts and appoint smaller committees. These, again, should at once devote themselves to volunteer patrol work at night as well as general detective service. The unfortunates who are the objects of the man-monster's malignity should be shadowed by one or two of the amateur patrols. They should be cautioned to walk in couples. Whistles and a signalling system should be provided.

This system of signalling, known as 'belling the cats', did not prove very popular among the 'cats' themselves. Another suggestion, that all prostitutes should be arrested after midnight, would have prevented one of the subsequent murders, at least.

One difficulty was the lack of decoys. There were no policewomen then and policemen had to dress up as women. This was another hilarious touch to contrast with the horror. An East Ender told me how his father had to dress up and was highly embarrassed because he sported a large black moustache which had to be shaved off. On one occasion an ambitious journalist dressed up as a woman in the hope of being accosted by the Ripper, but was stopped by a policeman instead, who asked: 'You're a man aren't you? Are you one of us?'

'I don't know what you mean,' replied the young journalist indignantly, 'but I'm not a copper if that's what you're referring to.'

The idea of Vigilance Committees caught on quickly. A statement was issued by a group of Whitechapel tradesmen two days after Chapman's murder: 'Finding that in spite of murders being committed in our midst, the police force is inadequate to discover the author or authors of the late atrocities, we, the undersigned, have formed ourselves into a committee and intend offering a substantial reward to any-one, citizen or otherwise, who shall give such information as will be the means of bringing the murderer or murderers to justice.' Vigilance Committees commanded immediate support and continued for some time to come. At the end of their plea for public committees of this sort, the *Star* concluded: 'We are not sure that every London district should not make an effort of the kind, for the murderer may choose a fresh quarter now that Whitechapel is being made too hot to hold him.'

It must have been thought inconceivable that the murderer should attack again in the same way in the same place. But on 30 September, the Ripper murdered again, and this time he claimed two victims within the night.

iii: *Double Event*

As Saturday became Sunday the Ripper met his first victim, Elizabeth Stride and they walked south of the crowded thoroughfare of Commercial Road. Many penniless prostitutes had no place of their own to take their clients and must have known every back-yard and alley intimately. This particular yard led to the back of 40 Berners Street, which was used by Russian and Polish Jews as an International Workers' Educational Club. On this night the wooden gates to the yard were left open and the sound of music and dancing came from the house, conveniently for the man and woman with their different objectives.

At one o'clock a hawker called Louis Diemschutz, who worked in the club at night as a part-time steward, drove into the yard with his pony and trap. The horse shied with alarm, probably from the smell of fresh blood, possibly because the murderer stood concealed in the entrance. The hawker jumped down to see what was wrong and noticed a bundle against the wall. This was Stride, the blood still pouring from her throat. The doctors discovered that her windpipe had been cut through and there were pressure marks on her shoulders, probably caused by the murderer's hands. But there were no mutilations: the Ripper had been interrupted. It is possible that as Diemschutz knelt by the corpse the Ripper slipped out of the yard and made his escape.

It was now Sunday morning, but there were still people about returning home from their Saturday night out. Imagine the Ripper's desperation: a sexual murderer deprived of his climax. He walked towards Aldgate, furious at the thought of what he might have done to the body if he had not been interrupted.

All too soon he was satisfied. A second body was discovered by PC Watkins in Mitre Square, a few minutes' walk away, at 1:45. His beat took fifteen minutes and he claimed he had seen nothing unusual at 1:30. The murder may have taken

34

place even earlier for an old map (see illustration no. 8) shows that another police constable lived in a corner house in Mitre Square opposite the scene of the murder, and it is at least possible that Watkins had been sipping a welcome cup of tea.

Certainly the Ripper had acted swiftly and taken a terrible revenge for his interruption a few minutes earlier. Watkins found the woman, Catherine Eddowes, lying on her back, the legs apart, her face gashed, her right eye damaged, the lower eyelids nicked, the lobe of her right ear missing, the intestines pulled out and laid over her right shoulder. 'I have been in the force a long while, but I never saw such a sight.' It was noticeable that with each murder, apart from the interruption with Stride, the Ripper became more abandoned.

Professor Francis Camps, the pathologist, and his assistant Sam Hardy, recently discovered sketches in the basement of the London Hospital in Whitechapel made by the doctor at the scene of the crime. Two of these sketches, the body on the ground and the body in the mortuary drawn by F. W. Foster at 3:45, suddenly put the name of the Ripper into horrifying focus. The body was *ripped* open – there is no other word for it. No wonder that the French call him 'Jacques L'Evrentreur' – Jack the stomach opener. Looking at the drawings and the police photographs, the whole question of expert medical knowledge becomes horrifyingly clear – the murderer must have plunged his fist into the body and pulled out what he desired with only the roughest idea of anatomy. Watkins compared the body to that of a pig ripped up for market.

Mitre Square lay within the jurisdiction of the City of London and Major Henry Smith, the active Commissioner of City Police, arrived on the scene in a hansom cab. Throughout that night he was a step behind the Ripper, who left a trail behind him. The Ripper had paused to wash the blood off his hands, in a public sink in a small passage, and left a blood-strained piece of Eddowes's apron in Goulston Street. Scrawled in chalk on a doorway nearby was a startling message that had not been there before: *The Jewes are not the men to be blamed for nothing.* As soon as Smith heard of this he sent an inspector to have it photographed, but this street was just outside his control and Sir Charles Warren intercepted him. Incredibly, Warren ordered the message to be rubbed out before any record could be taken, and may even have done this himself. The suggestion that he did this to avoid an outburst of anti-semitism does not excuse the blunder. The meaning of the message remains a mystery – perhaps deliberately misleading, perhaps some oblique reference to the interruption by the Jew earlier in the evening, perhaps some chance scribble by someone else altogether.

This episode accentuated the animosity between the City Police and the Metropolitan Police. Unlike Warren, who was a teetotaller, Major Smith had put a third of his men into plain clothes since August and deliberately encouraged them to hang around pubs learning all the gossip they could. It must have exasperated him further when he learnt that Catherine Eddowes had been arrested only a few hours earlier.

Eddowes fitted the pattern of the other women, drunk and middle-aged, forty-three though she looked sixty, but she had just enjoyed the respite of a few days hop-picking in the country. This was a favourite cockney pastime, earning a little money while providing a sort of holiday. She returned to London on the Thursday with the man she was living with, John Kelly; it has been claimed that they hoped to raise the reward by identifying the Ripper, but this is fanciful and unsubstantiated.

By Friday the couple were so poor they had to separate, sharing sixpence that Kelly had earned – fourpence for him in a doss-house, twopence for her in the squalour of the Casual Ward in Mile End Road. On the Saturday she went to borrow money from her daughter and might have been successful for she was seen at eight o'clock staggering in the middle of the road imitating a fire-engine. She was arrested and held in the Bishopsgate Police Station under the name of 'Kate Kelly'. She sobered up around midnight and unluckily she was allowed to leave at one o'clock. 'Ta-ta, old cock,' she is supposed to have said to the Duty-Sergeant, 'I'll see you again soon.' She was dead within minutes. Major Smith had given orders that every man and woman seen together after midnight had to be accounted for. He wrote afterwards: 'Had she been followed, and men called to guard the approaches, the murderer would to a certainty have been taken red-handed.'

A description of her clothes, after the body had been taken to the Mortuary in Golden Lane, gives an idea of her appearance: 'She wore a black cloth jacket with imitation fur collar and three large metal buttons. Her dress is of dark green print, the pattern consisting of Michaelmas daisies and golden lilies. She also wore a thin white vest, a drab linsey skirt, and a very dark green alpaca petticoat, white chemise and brown ribbed stockings mended at the foot with white material.' Her black straw bonnet was trimmed with black beads, and black and green velvet. Round her neck was a piece of ribbon and, rather curiously, 'a piece of old white coarse apron'. She wore a pair of man's boots on her feet. Her possessions were many but pathetic: a piece of string; a 'common' white handkerchief; a blunt table knife; a match box with cotton in it; two clay pipes; a red cigarette case; five pieces of soap; a small box with tea and sugar; 'a portion' of a pair of spectacles; a small comb, a red mitten and a ball of worsted.

The body was not identified until 2 October, the Tuesday, by John Kelly. Further identification came from a tin box with two pawnbrokers' tickets in the names of Emily Burrell and Anne Kelly. They were for a man's boots and flannel shirt, pledged for 1s. 6d. each.

It seems surprising, in view of the tension in the East End, that the Ripper should have been able to pick women up with such ease as he did with Stride and Eddowes. Eddowes was in need of money, but she had sobered up and must have felt a natural suspicion of any stranger accosting her, yet she went readily to her death in the dark corner of the square. One may reasonably make certain deductions: either the murderer was not a stranger, or he was someone who commanded immediate confidence, like a clergyman or a policeman; or, at least, he seemed respectable. This is inference, but it does seem reasonable to assume that he was not the swarthy foreigner, the 'leather apron' that had seized the imagination.

Elizabeth Stride was another prostitute, aged forty-five. She was known as 'Long Liz' and had married a carpenter called Thomas Stride in 1869; her maiden name was Gustafsdotter and she came from Sweden. In 1878 the steamer *Princess Alice* sank in the Thames and her husband and two of her nine children were drowned. She was rescued – or so she claimed, for East Enders were still emotional over the tragedy in which several hundred people lost their lives, and such a story could have commanded sympathy. She ended up in lodgings in Flower and Dean Street, notorious for its prostitutes even in that district, and was frequently arrested for drunkenness.

Three witnesses claimed to have seen her shortly before the murder. A labourer called Marshall, who lived in Berners Street, said he saw Stride kissing a man for nearly ten minutes, around 12:45. A man called Brown passed by at about the same time and heard Stride say, 'Not tonight, but some other night'. The constable on the beat also saw her with a man, but their descriptions varied and finally the Police Gazette issued two descriptions, though they were probably of the same man:

'At 12:35 a.m., 30 September, with Elizabeth Stride found murdered on the same date in Berners Street at 1 a.m., a man age twenty-eight, height five feet eight inches, complexion, dark, small dark moustache; dress, black diagonal coat, hard felt hat, collar and tie, respectable appearance, carried a parcel wrapped up in newspaper.'

'At 12:45 a.m., 30 September, with the same woman in Berners Street, a man, aged about thirty, height five feet five inches; complexion fair, hair dark, small brown moustache, full face, broad shoulders; dress, dark jacket and trousers, black cap with peak.'

A German came forward to say he had seen Eddowes with a man shortly before her death. The *Police Gazette* issued another notice:

'At 1:35 a.m., 30 September, with Catherine Eddowes, in

Church Passage leading to Mitre Square, where she was found murdered at 1:45 a.m., a man age thirty, height five feet, seven or eight inches; complexion fair, moustache fair, medium build; dress: pepper and salt colour loose jacket, grey cloth cap with peak of same material, reddish neckerchief tied in knot; appearance of a sailor.'

The most interesting common factor is the age, placed around thirty.

The Ripper was lucky in the vagueness of the descriptions, for the murders did not take place in a thick winter fog as the films would suggest. He was lucky too that the night watchman of Kearley and Tonge's factory, on the side of Mitre Square, had not been standing outside for his usual smoke and chat with PC Watkins. Instead he was busy inside the warehouse and, as I have suggested, Watkins may well have been in the house of his colleague opposite.

Even so, the Ripper worked with speed. When the body was examined by four doctors at the mortuary in Golden Lane, Dr Sequiera, who arrived at the square only ten minutes after Watkins found the body, said the killing could only have taken three minutes. Dr Brown insisted that some surgical skill would have been required. The reason he said this was that a kidney had been removed. Gradually, the police began to realise that this kidney presented an all-important clue to the identity of 'Jack the Ripper' as he was to be known from now on.

The police released a letter that had been sent to the editor of the Central News Agency two days before the double-murder. The name of Jack the Ripper appeared for the first time:

Dear Boss,

I keep on hearing the police have caught me but they won't fix me just yet. I have laughed when they look so clever and talk about being on the right track. The joke about Leather Apron gave me real fits.

I am down on whores and I shan't quit ripping them till I do get buckled. Grand work, the last job was. I gave the

39

lady no time to squeal. How can they catch me now? I love my work and want to start again. You will soon hear of me and my funny little games.

I saved some of the proper red stuff in a ginger beer bottle over the last job, to write with, but it went thick like glue and I can't use it. Red ink is fit enough I hope. Ha! Ha!

The next job I do I shall clip the lady's ears off and send to the police officers just for jolly wouldn't you. Keep this letter back till I do a bit more work, then give it out straight. My knife is nice and sharp I want to get to work right away if I get a chance. Good luck.

Yours truly.

Jack the Ripper.

Don't mind me giving the trade name, wasn't good enough to post this before I got all the red ink off my hands curse it. No luck yet they say I am a doctor now ha ha.

This was followed by a postcard written and posted on Sunday 30 September, a few hours after the double-murder. Plainly it was a follow-up:

I was not codding dear old Boss when I gave you the tip. You'll hear about Saucy Jack's work tomorrow. Double event this time. Number one squealed a bit. Couldn't finish straight off. Had not time to get ears for police. Thanks for keeping last letter back till I got to work again.

Jack the Ripper.

The letter and the postcard were reproduced on a Metropolitan Police poster on 3 October, with the statement at the bottom: 'Any person recognising the handwriting is requested to communicate with the nearest Police Station.' The police had every reason for taking them seriously. No details about the double murder were published until Monday in the morning papers, yet the card referred to a 'double event'. The writer could have learnt this by word of mouth, but 'Number one squealed a bit' could well have been a reference to a cry heard by a woman who was standing in a doorway in Berners Street at the time Stride was being killed, and the reference to the ears was even more significant for Eddowes's ears had been cut, though not severed. In releasing the communications, publicising the Ripper's macabre sense of humour and swaggering self-confidence, the police inflamed the imagination of the people of the East End.

Even given the difficulty of their task, the heads of police were curiously insensitive. An Assistant Commissioner called Monro had resigned because he felt unable to work with Sir Charles Warren, and was replaced by Sir Robert Anderson. Unfortunately Anderson was none too well and spent the first month of his appointment in Switzerland, though he did make the concession of cutting this short and spending the last week in Paris in order to be nearer to Scotland Yard.

Much later, in *The Lighter Side of my Official Life*, he had the gall to write: 'When the stolid English go in for a scare they take leave of all moderation and common sense. If nonsense were solid, the nonsense that was talked and written about these murders would sink a Dreadnought.' Like many government officials who resent criticism, he blamed the press. Writing in *Criminals and Crime* he claimed that, 'At the time the sensation-mongers of the newspaper press fostered the belief that life in London was no longer safe, and that no woman ought to venture abroad in the streets after nightfall, and one enterprising journalist went so far as to impersonate the cause of all this terror as '*Jack the Ripper*', the name by which he will probably go down in history. But no amount of silly hysteria could alter the fact that these crimes were a cause of danger only to a particular section of a small and definite class of woman in a limited district of the East End.'

It *is* possible that the communications were the hoax of an enterprising journalist. Sir Melville Macnaghten agreed with this: 'I have always thought I could discern the stained forefinger of the journalist – indeed, a year later I had shrewd suspicions as to the actual author! But whoever did pen the gruesome stuff, it is certain to my mind that it was not the mad

41

miscreant who had committed the murders.' But even if they were a hoax, which is far from certain, it was the police and not the press who gave them maximum publicity. Certainly there was hysteria, but it shows the complacency of Anderson that he could call it 'silly' long after the event. It was not 'silly' then, because it was there. It was an epidemic.

Though the press did not create it, it is true that they took every advantage of the sensation in making it still more sensational. They wallowed in the purple prose of a 'Penny Dreadful': 'Horror ran throughout the land. Men spoke of it with bated breath, and pale-lipped women shuddered as they read the dreadful details. People afar off smelt blood, and the superstitious said that the skies had been of a deeper red that Autumn.'

Hoardings became so gruesome that they were denounced by *Punch*: 'Imagine the effect of these gigantic pictures of violence and assassination ... on the morbid imagination of imbalanced minds.' Newspaper boys had a field-day. 'No one who was living in London that Autumn will forget the terror created by these murders,' wrote Sir Melville Macnaghten. 'Even now I remember the foggy evenings and the cries of the newspaper boys, "Another horrible murder, murder, mutilation, Whitechapel." ' In November the *Daily Telegraph* published a letter of protest:

Sir,

Can nothing be done to prevent a set of hoarse ruffians coming nightly about our suburban squares and streets yelling at the tops of their hideous voices: 'Special Edition – Whitechapel Murder – Another of 'em – Mutilation – Special Edition – beautiful – awful – Murder!' and so on, and nearly frightening the life out of the sensitive women and children of the neighbourhood?

Last evening, for instance, their cry was 'Special! – Murder – Paper – The Ripper – Caught'. These awful words were bawled out about nine o'clock in a quiet part of Kensington; a lady who was supping with us was so greatly distressed by these hideous bellowings that she was absolutely too unnerved to return home save in a cab because she would have to walk about a hundred or two yards down a quiet street at the end of her journey by omnibus.

Now, I venture to ask, sir, is it not monstrous that the police do not protect us from such flagrant and ghastly nuisances? I enclose my card and beg to subscribe myself,

Pembroke Square.

It is claimed that a Mrs Mary Burridge was so distressed when she read the newspaper account of the murder of Annie Chapman that she had a fit and died, with the late edition clasped in her hand.

A publican in Whitechapel blamed his bankruptcy on the empty streets at night; 'People aren't going out any more,' he explained, 'Since the killings I hardly get a soul in here of a night.' This was confirmed by a letter to *The Times*: 'I and a friend, last night made a tour of the district ... and in spite of what we had been led to believe, found the district almost deserted. We walked through street after street without meeting a soul.'

Of particular interest was the surge of sympathy felt towards the people of the East End by the West End. As a gesture, the American actor Richard Mansfield withdrew his production of *Dr Jekyll and Mr Hyde* from the Lyceum in October after a run of only ten weeks. Far from exploiting the situation, he gave a final benefit performance to raise money especially for the homeless of the East End. 'Experience has taught this clever young actor that there is no taste in London just now for horrors on the stage,' declared the *Daily Telegraph* solemnly. 'There is quite sufficient to make us shudder out of doors.'

A few days after the 'Ripper' letters were published by the police, another was sent to a builder called George Lusk, the Chairman of the Whitechapel Vigilance Committee (see illustration no. 13). It was enclosed in a small cardboard box, and on top of the note there was the sinister or poignant address: *From hell*.

Mr Lusk

Sir I send you half the Kidne I took from one woman prasarved it for you, tother piece I fried and ate it was very nice. I may send you the bloody knif that took it out if you only wate a whil longer

Signed Catch me when you can

Mister Lusk

This is the most important of all the letters, and it is interesting to note that the writer did not use the signature of 'Jack the Ripper'. It contains various points of significance, which I shall discuss later when I examine the handwriting. There is every reason to believe that this letter came from the 'Ripper'.

Though the enclosure of the kidney was treated as a macabre joke by most of the newspapers, it was taken seriously by Dr Openshaw, a pathologist at the London Hospital, for he believed that it had come from the body of Catherine Eddowes. It had been taken within the last two weeks from a woman of about forty-five: she was forty-three; it was gin sodden: gin had been her favourite drink; the kidney showed an advanced state of Bright's disease: Eddowes was suffering from Bright's disease. An inch of renal artery was attached to the kidney and this is of special importance for the artery is three inches long altogether and two inches had been left in the body, making it complete. A colleague agreed that the kidney had been placed in spirits within a few hours of its removal. It would seem beyond coincidence.

There are two other letters which are relevant, as I shall explain. These came from Liverpool and the first was sent the day before the double-murder: 'Beware, I shall be at work on the 1st and 2nd Inst. in Minories at twelve midnight, and I give the authorities a good chance, but there is never a policeman near when I am at work. Yours, Jack the Ripper.' This was too prophetic and close for comfort; he was out by only twenty-three hours and a few hundred yards. Another letter came from Prince William Street in Liverpool: 'What fools the police are. I even give them the name of the street where I am living. Yours, Jack the Ripper.' This too is important.

Major Smith had the sense not to ignore these letters, as his colleagues did. He believed the kidney came from Eddowes, and personally received a further letter on the subject: 'you was rite it was the lift kidny; i was goin to hopperate again close to your ospittle – ust as i was going to drop my nife along of er bloomin throte them cusses of coppers spoilt the game but i guess i will be on the job soon and will send you another bit of innerds. Jack the Ripper.' Altogether hundreds of letters were received sent by different people and many were transparent and sometimes even entertaining hoaxes.

One of the first documents to confront Sir Melville Macnaghten when he took office was the following verse:

> I'm not a butcher,
> I'm not a Yid,
> Nor yet a foreign skipper,
> But I'm your own light-hearted friend,
> Yours truly, Jack the Ripper.

Many communications were in this form; another rhyme was all the more sinister for being well-composed: It refers to Gladstone's habit of befriending women of the street in the hope of reforming them:

Eight little whores, with no hope of heaven,
Gladstone may save one, then there'll be seven.
Seven little whores begging for a shilling,
One stays in Henage Court, then there's a killing.
Six little whores, glad to be alive.
One sidles up to Jack, then there are five.
Four and whore rhyme aright,
So do three and me,
I'll set the town alight
Ere there are two.

Two little whores, shivering with fright,
Seek a cosy doorway in the middle of the night.
Jack's knife flashes, then there's but one,
And the last one's the ripest for Jack's idea of fun.

Meanwhile, in spite of the clues and the tiny area in which the Ripper operated, the police floundered without success. The clamour grew for the resignation of Sir Charles Warren. London held its breath and waited.

iv: *Mary Kelly*

The Ripper's final victim Mary Kelly, or Marie Jeanette Kelly as she fancied herself, was attractive, lively and twenty-five years old. Otherwise she was a drunken prostitute like the others. Born in Ireland, she had married at sixteen and moved to Cardiff after her husband's death in a mining accident. Then she enjoyed a slight success in the West End of London and it is claimed that she went to Paris for a short time to live as the mistress of one of her clients.

Now she was on the inevitable 'road to ruin', though she was able to rent a small room at 13 Miller's Court for four shillings a week from the landlord John M'Carthy. She shared this room with a labourer called Joseph Barnet, until the end of October when she wanted to bring home another prostitute, Mrs Harvey, to live with them. Not surprisingly Barnet objected to this and walked out after a row in which one of their windows was broken. Maria Harvey stayed in the room a couple of nights and was there on Thursday afternoon, 8 November, when Barnet looked in to see if Kelly was all right. That was the last time he saw her.

However, so many people saw Mary Kelly that night, or claimed to see her, that her movements, far from being clear, became most confusing. One thing is certain: she was behind with her rent and desperate for money.

Thursday 10:30 p.m.: A woman met Kelly, who said that unless she was able to get money she'd kill herself. Kelly was seen to walk off with a man.

11:45 p.m: Mary Cox who lived in Miller's Court, saw Kelly, who was rather drunk, with a short, stout man.

Midnight: Mary Cox heard Kelly singing 'Only a violet I plucked for my mother's grave,' and saw a light in her room.

Friday 2:00 a.m: An out-of-work labourer, George Hutchinson, was walking down Whitechapel Road into Commercial Street. He noticed a man on the corner of Thrawl Street, and walking on towards the next corner of Flower and Dean Street he met Mary Kelly whom he knew. She asked him to lend her sixpence, but even this sum was beyond him. With a smile Kelly said she'd have to find it somewhere else and moved on towards Thrawl Street where she met the man on the corner. She spoke to him, he put his hand on her shoulder, they laughed and walked off together, passing Hutchinson on their way, presumably to Miller's Court. 'My suspicions were instantly aroused,' he said later, 'at seeing so well-dressed a man in this part of London. I felt there was something queer about it.' Because he was envious, or just plain curious, Hutchinson followed them across Dorset Street towards Miller's Court and actually waited there for three-quarters of an hour to see if they came out again.

At 2:30 a.m. Sara Lewis a Spitalfield's laundress, saw a man outside No. 13. This might have been Hutchinson. Hutchinson's description of the man was detailed, though a soft hat was pulled down over the man's eyes. He said he was five feet six, around thirty-four or thirty-five years old, with a dark moustache twirled at the ends. He wore a long coat trimmed with astrakhan, a horseshoe pin in his necktie, dark spats with light buttons, a watch-chain with a seal and red stone, and he carried a thin parcel in his left hand, about eight inches long, covered with dark American cloth. His description might seem almost too good. But Hutchinson believed he had seen the man before, in Petticoat Lane Market on a Sunday morning. Hutchinson left around three o'clock.

3:00 a.m: At this time, the doctors testified later, Mary Kelly was being killed.

3:30 a.m: Sarah Lewis heard the cry of 'Murder!' and saw a faint light in Kelly's room.

3:40 a.m: Mrs Prater, who lived in 20 Miller's Court, also heard the faint cry of 'Murder!'. Presumably this was the same cry, if both women were telling the truth.

6:00 a.m: Mary Cox heard a man's footsteps leaving the Court.

8:00 a.m: A tailor claimed to have seen Kelly.

8:30 a.m: A neighbour, Mrs Maxwell, not only claimed that she saw Kelly, but even spoke to her at the corner of Miller's Court.

9:00 a.m: Mrs Maxwell saw Kelly talking to a man.

10:00 a.m: Another witness claims to have seen Mary Kelly. You will notice that Mary Kelly was seen to be alive after she was dead. This merely confirms what the police always say, that eye-witnesses are notoriously unreliable.

10:45 a.m: John Bowyer, a messenger for the landlord John M'Carthy was sent to collect the rent that was owed by Mary Kelly, with instructions from M'Carthy that this was her last chance. Bowyer knocked on the door of 13 Miller's Court. When there was no sound, he reached through the broken window and pulled the muslin curtains apart. When Bowyer saw Mary Kelly on her bed he ran to M'Carthy who called the police.

All the Ripper murders were violent, but the murder of Mary Kelly was peculiarly abandoned. This time he didn't rip the body apart, he sliced her as if he was a butcher preparing trays of meat for his window. On the mattress lay a mass of raw flesh; her throat was cut from ear to ear, though in fact the ears and the nose were missing; the face destroyed; the liver removed; and there was a display of kidneys, heart and slices of the victim's breasts laid out on a bedside table. It was a bloodbath. There were bloodstains on the wall and pieces of flesh dripped from the picture-rails. The crime is bad enough to read about, but must have been terrible to see. John M'Carthy said at the time: 'I cannot drive away from my mind the sight we saw. I had heard a great deal about the Whitechapel murders, but I declare to God I had never expected to see such a sight as this. The whole scene is more than I can describe.'

When the police arrived, Inspector Beck looked through the window and urged the young detective with him (who became famous later as the Chief Inspector Dew who arrested Crippen), 'For God's sake, Dew, don't look.' But Dew looked all the same: 'What I saw when I pushed back an old coat and peeped through a broken pane of glass into the sordid little room which Kelly called her home was too harrowing to be described. It remains with me – and always will remain – as the most grue-some memory of the whole of my police career.'

To make it even more macabre, the surrounding streets were thronged with people heading cheerfully towards the Lord Mayor's Show. The police were mesmerised. Commissioner Warren had given orders that any further murder site was not to be touched until bloodhounds could be brought there, so policemen were ordered not to enter the room. They waited until eight o'clock in the evening when they learnt that Sir Charles Warren had resigned the night before and had been replaced by Sir Robert Anderson. Now Superintendent Arnold at last gave the order to break down the door, and a photograph was taken. This extraordinary photograph is reproduced here for the first time. Sir Melville Macnaghten referred to it later: 'The murderer must have taken at least two hours over his hellish job. A photograph was taken at the time ... without seeing which it is impossible to understand or grasp the extent of the awful mutilation.'

Lady Aberconway, Sir Melville's daughter, told me that when she was a child he took her to Scotland Yard one Sunday after church. Suddenly all hell broke loose as she was dis-covered looking through some photographs which had been left unlocked and were snatched away. 'But to me,' she said, 'the mutilated bodies looked just like broken dolls!' These were the photographs of the Ripper's victims, which are reproduced here for the first time.

A photographer took a photo of Mary Kelly's eyes in the belief that the last image seen is retained on the retina. This theory is conveyed, horribly, in Rudyard Kipling's strange and brilliant short story, *At the End of the Passage*. But nothing was found. This was one of the final acts of Sir Charles Warren – before his resignation became effective on 12 November, when it was greeted with cheers in the House of Commons – along with this offer:

'MURDER PARDON. Whereas, on 8 or 9 November in Miller's Court, Dorset Street, Spitalfields, Mary Jane Kelly was murdered by some person or persons unknown, the Secretary of State will advise the grant of Her Majesty's pardon to any accomplice not being a person who contrived or actually committed the murder who shall give such information and evidence as shall lead to the discovery and conviction of the person or persons who committed the murder.

'Charles Warren. Commissioner of Police of the Metropolis."

The clues contained in the room at Miller's Court were curious. Kelly's clothes were laid at the foot of her bed, but ashes in the fire-grate revealed the remains of a bonnet and some velvet. The handle and spout of the kettle had melted, or disintegrated so the fire must have been fierce indeed. The key was gone, but one report said the door was bolted from the inside.

Five doctors examined the body before it was placed in a black 'shell' and taken to Shoreditch Mortuary on a public deathcart drawn by a horse driven by a pauper. Several small parcels contained the bits of the body. In the mortuary it took them six hours to reassemble Kelly into the semblance of a human being.

Because the Shoreditch Mortuary was outside the jurisdiction of Mr Baxter, who had proved antagonistic to the police on the previous occasions, the inquest was handled by another coroner and a verdict was reached with a haste that obliterated all serious evidence. The authorities were doing their utmost to 'play down' the sensation as far as possible, for the East

End crowds were close to rioting and anyone who seemed even faintly suspicious was in danger of his life.

Mary Kelly's funeral took place on 18 November; several thousand people gathered outside Shoreditch Church. There were three large wreaths on the coffin and the mourners went to Leytonstone cemetery in two coachloads, among them was Joseph Barnet. The cost of the interment was paid for by a Mr Wilton, the clerk of the church. He suggested that if the public wished to share in the expense they could send their subscriptions to him. If there was any surplus, a tombstone would be erected; there was no tombstone.

I heard of a curious incident which took place in the cemetery that afternoon. The mother of the person who wrote to me was visiting another grave. After the mourners for Kelly had gone, she and her friend noticed that one man stayed behind and after some time, believing himself to be alone, he parted the boards above the grave and spat down on it while the terrified women hid behind their tombstone. I asked my informant whether they had told the police: 'They were too scared. They thought the Ripper might take revenge on them.' Such stories, of course, are hearsay, but they illustrate the feeling about the Ripper at the time.

This was the Ripper's last act of murder. Referring to the pregnancy of Kelly and the discovery of a three-month old foetus in the womb, Colin Wilson asks: 'Was this, perhaps, an ultimate thrill? His psychosis had something to do with a horror of birth; now he had destroyed a baby as well as the mother.' The Ripper could go no further. If there was any objective, he had reached it. If an obsession, it must have been fulfilled. 'To my way of thinking,' wrote Sir Melville Macnaghten afterwards, 'the Ripper's brain gave way altogether after his awful glut [in Miller's Court] and he committed suicide.'

Although they disposed of the inquest on Kelly as speedily as possible the police could not conceal the gruesome details. On 10 November the *Star* published an account which needed no embroidery: 'The ears and nose had been cut clean off; the breasts had also been cut cleanly off and placed on a table which was by the side of the bed. The stomach and abdomen had been ripped open, while the face was slashed about . . .'

Inevitably there was anger in the East End. Many people were threatened by the public and arrested by the police. But then, as if the people were numbed by so much violence, or sensed somehow that the Ripper could go no further, a sort of calm descended. Senior Inspectors and policemen assigned especially to the case were withdrawn. Though scares and arrests of suspects continued, there was not that additional panic one might have expected.

But there was one sensation later in the month on Wednesday the 21, when a further letter was received from 'Jack the Ripper' by Mr Saunders, the sitting magistrate at the Thames Police Court.

> Dear Boss, It is no use for you to look for me in London because I'm not there. Don't trouble yourself about me until I return, which will not be very long. I like the work too well to leave it alone. Oh, it was a jolly job the last one. I had plenty of time to do it properly in. Ha, Ha, Ha! The next lot I mean to do with Vengeance, cut of their head and arms. You think it is a man with a black moustache. Ha, ha, ha! When I have done another one you can try and catch me again. So goodbye dear Boss, till I return.
> Yours,
> Jack the Ripper.

The postmark on the envelope was Portsmouth. When I investigated further I realised the extent to which the Ripper had seized the imagination, though this was the final epidemic. Understandably, the letter created a panic in Portsmouth – but the letter was not the only cause of this. That same morning, a tradesman in Portsea, opening his shop, found the name *Jack the Ripper* scrawled in chalk across the shutters. This triggered off false alarms, like the report of a burglary from a landlady who claimed that the 'men-intruders' were 'Jack the Ripper', until it was discovered they were friends of her new lady lodger. Several well-known residents in Havant received letters signed 'Jack the Ripper'. Mr Lockyer, a postmaster, reported two such letters – one left in a plain envelope in a draper's shop containing a rough illustration of a man brandishing a knife in his hand, striking at a woman who is exclaiming 'Oh dear!' At the top of the sketch was the message: 'Mr Lockyer, I am not Jack the Ripper but I am Jack the Ripper's pal. I have done a murder or two, but the next one I intend to do will be a woman at Emsworth. Look out.' The other letter contained sketches of Sir Charles Warren, the Home Secretary and some policemen, with the warning, 'We intend to get the best of them.' The Portsmouth *Times* commented: 'Of course these sensational missives are in all probability the handiwork of some leisured idiot who thinks he is playing off a capital practical joke.'

But fantasy became fact with the tragedy of Monday the 26: 'A murder, scarcely less horrible in its atrocity, in its brutal callousness, and its mysterious character than the White-chapel murders was perpetrated at the Pallant, Havant,' reported the Portsmouth *Times*, fanning the alarm with the comparison. 'An inoffensive, dark-haired, fresh-complexioned lad of eight summers, who is said to have been bright, cheerful and intelligent, was murdered by an unknown man. Though there is at present no clue to the perpetrator of the horrible deed or to the motive, it is clear that the crime was not pre-meditated. The foul deed was clumsily perpetrated, a blunt knife being the weapon used, and the assassin flung away the implement with which he had wrought the death of a school-boy, who had, so far as can be ascertained, never done him any wrong, and then decamped.' The gash had severed the jugular vein under the right ear, and there were further cuts. The boy was called Percy Searle and his father was a bricklayer's labourer who fainted when he heard the news and remained un-conscious for several hours. Writing about the boy, in the curious journalistic style of the time, the Portsmouth *Times* said, 'He may have had his faults, but they could not have been great, as the most careful enquiry in the neighbourhood of the murder last night failed to elicit anything derogatory to the boy's character. The worst that could be said of him was that he was passionately fond of his parents, his lessons, and his everyday associates. The motive for the crime, if any, is for the present known only to the murderer himself. It was reported on Monday that boys have gone about pretending to be 'Jack the Ripper', but no boy could have inflicted on his equal in strength such terrible wounds as caused the death of Percy Searle.'

The only eye-witness was an eleven-year-old boy called Husband 'who was near the Manor House school shortly after six o'clock on Monday, when he saw, in the feeble light reflected by a lamp, a man struggling with a boy. Searle uttered the most piteous cries, but Husband, anxious to obtain timely help, ran towards Mr Platt, a milkman, whose well-known lamp led Husband to identify him, and these two simultaneously made a most ghastly discovery.' Husband saw a 'tall thin man' running away, and another report quoted him as saying that he wore a top hat and was carrying a black bag – the conventional image of the Ripper. A possible clue was the bloodstained, ordinary 'buck-handled pocket knife' discovered by the headmaster of the local school. The blade was blunt, suggesting that exceptional force had been used.

Robbery could hardly have been the motive, and the Portsmouth *Times* hinted that 'the murderer attempted to commit another crime, not unknown in Assize calendars, and that he stopped the boy's cries by resorting to the knife'. But another report referred to a total absence of any motive, which led the Havant residents to 'connect the unknown murderer with the shadowy miscreant who is popularly known as "Jack the Ripper". There is not, of course, the slightest evidence to justify the belief that the same hand which has been at its deadly work in the slums of the East End of London among the fallen sisterhood is guilty of the strange and unnatural offence which it is our duty to chronicle today; but a good deal of emphasis is laid on the fact that a few days since a letter bearing the signature of "Jack the Ripper" was received in London with the Portsmouth postmark upon it, and this document is being quoted as proof conclusive that the Whitechapel murderer has visited this county.'

This is a case which it is necessary to explore if only to dismiss any connection between it and the Whitechapel murders. It is conceivable that the letter was sent by the genuine Ripper, and probable that the murder was one of imitation, but the two were not the act of the same hand. On 1 December the Portsmouth *Times* reported 'the arrest of the lad Husband yesterday afternoon on the grave charge of wilful murder'. It was alleged that the murderer was the other boy, the only eye-witness. Apparently this 'did not come altogether as a surprise, but it was nevertheless a great relief to the inhabitants of the district for, as was only natural under the circumstances, the idea has got abroad that the terrible being who has perpetrated the undiscovered murders in the East End of London had made his appearance at Havant...'

Husband was sent for trial at Winchester Assizes, for there was no juvenile court in those days, and remanded in custody. It was established that the murder knife was his, that he had been seen with the victim just before the murder, and was the only person to have 'witnessed' the killer – yet, surprisingly, he was found not guilty and acquitted. At this distance one can only wonder. But the episode reveals the obsession with the Ripper that persisted in November, though it died down afterwards. Possibly the country outside London had a delayed reaction. 'The mere suggestion that Jack the Ripper might have been the culprit in the present instance threw the whole neighbourhood for miles into a state of violent excitement, which increased rather than subsided as time passed without news of an arrest,' wrote the Portsmouth *Times*. 'Terror-stricken women and children, and in some cases even grown-up men, were timorous of venturing out alone in secluded places after nightfall, and all spoke with bated breath of the gruesome deed which causes a thrill of horror throughout the country . . .'

This illustrates, further, how any murder which bore the slightest resemblance to the Whitechapel murders, was attributed to the Ripper over the next few years. The following women are sometimes claimed as his further victims:

Alice McKenzie was found with her throat cut in Castle Alley, Aldgate on 17 July 1889. Castle Alley was a thin passage with such a bad reputation that people were afraid to go there at night in case they were robbed or attacked, but a policeman found McKenzie there, her throat stabbed and stomach slashed, at 12:50 on a Wednesday morning. She was also known as 'Clay-Pipe Alice' because she smoked a clay pipe in bed; indeed such a pipe was found underneath her body. The man she lived with said she was respectable, but the police thought differently and knew she solicited men. No arrests were made.

Frances Cole was murdered on 13 February 1891. PC Leeson heard a police-whistle and ran to Swallow Gardens where he found two colleagues who were looking at a body and told him: 'A Jack the Ripper job.' Leeson described the form in the road as that of a young woman: 'Her clothing was disarranged, and there could be no doubt that she had been brutally murdered. Apart from the fearful wound in the throat there were terrible injuries about the lower part of the trunk.' Cole was still alive but dying fast. Leeson recognised her as a prostitute called 'Carroty Nell' who came from Thrawl Street in Spitalfields, where Kelly is supposed to have met the man who killed her. She was young and pretty for a woman of her type. This time there were definite clues. A shopkeeper testified she had sold the hat that Cole was wearing, only the day before. At first she hadn't enough money, but she returned in the afternoon with a man who waited outside the shop while she paid the few shillings. A man had gone to her lodgings that same evening and when it was noticed that his hand was bleeding he explained he had just been attacked and robbed. He left around 1:00. Cole left half an hour later and was killed. The man returned to the lodgings around 3 : 00 and this time he was covered with blood. He said he had been knocked down for the second time and robbed in Ratcliffe Highway. The keeper didn't believe this and refused him a bed in the doss-house, telling him to go to the London Hospital. Sure enough, the police discovered that a man had reported there and left after treatment.

The doctors said he was a seaman. Leeson recorded: 'There was tremendous excitement now among the police engaged on the case, as it really looked as though they were hot on the trail of the Terror. Next day the excitement spread to the people outside, and big crowds assembled in front of Leman Street police station waiting for the news that Jack the Ripper had been laid by the heels at last.'

After such an interval there was curiosity rather than anxiety. Boys and girls clustered round the site of the murder, lighting matches to look at the police mark on the wall nearby. A piano-organ was dragged to the spot and they danced around it, improvising songs about the Ripper.

Meanwhile the ships were watched and a man was noticed at the dock gates and followed to a pub in Whitechapel where he was arrested. He was Thomas Sadler, a fireman off the SS *Fez*, moored in the London docks. He admitted buying Cole the hat and having been with her that evening. Everything, and everyone, pointed to his guilt, but he insisted his innocence and appealed for help to the Stokers' Union: 'What a godsend my case will be to the police,' he wrote, 'if they can only conduct me, innocent as I am, to the bitter end – the scaffold!'

The union representative defended him well and discovered that Sadler had been attacked twice that night. The magistrate concerned consulted the Attorney General, and Sadler was released by the police. It is said that he collected damages from a newspaper which had libelled him as the murderer, signed on for a ship bound for South America, and disappeared. The *Spectator* commented: 'It is almost beyond doubt that, black as the evidence against Sadler originally looked, he did not kill the woman; and it is more than possible, it is almost probable, that she was killed by "Jack the Ripper", as the populace have nicknamed the systematic murderer of prostitutes in Whitechapel.'

The police thought no such thing. In his private notes, Sir Melville Macnaghten indicted Sadler: 'He was a man of ungovernable temper, and entirely addicted to drink and the company of the lowest prostitutes. I have *no doubt* whatever in my own mind as to his having murdered Frances Cole.' Mcnaghten implied further that Sadler had murdered Alice McKenzie as well: 'The stab in the throat was identically the same,' and, 'It was subsequently ascertained that Sadler had sailed for the Baltic on 19 July 1889 and was in Whitechapel on the 17, the night that Alice McKenzie was killed.'

Colin Wilson has an intriguing alternative solution to the murder of Cole: General Booth of the Salvation Army had a secretary who was troubled by 'dreams of blood'. One day he told Booth that 'Carroty Nell will be the next to go'. After the murder he disappeared. (The source for this was an old article in *Tit Bits*). Another suspect was Thomas Cutbush who escaped from the Lambeth Infirmary on 5 March 1891 and was rearrested four days later on several charges of stabbing. A clerk in the Minories, he had contracted syphilis in 1888, after which his brain had become affected. The *Sun* newspaper revived the Ripper scare by claiming that his knife was similiar to that used in the earlier murders. Macnaghten dismissed the connection, proving that the knife had been bought recently, 'two years and three months *after* the last Whitechapel murder was committed'. Cutbush was found to be insane and was sentenced to be detained during Her Majesty's pleasure. The Ripper continued to be blamed for murders all over the world, regardless of evidence. Gradually this subsided and by the end of the century he became part of history.

Of all the other alleged victims of the Ripper, Martha Turner is perhaps the most likely. But Sir Melville was convinced that there were five Ripper murders only, all in 1888. Let us recapitulate them:

31 August: Mary Nicholls, found in Bucks Row, her throat cut and slight mutilations to the stomach;

8 September: Annie Chapman found in a backyard at Hanbury Street, throat cut and bad mutilation as to stomach and private parts;

30 September: Elizabeth Stride, throat cut only, Berners Street;

30 September: Catherine Eddowes, found in Mitre Square, throat cut, bad mutilations of face, stomach and private parts;

9 November: Mary Kelly, found in a room in Miller's Court, with throat cut and the *whole* face and body fiendishly mutilated.

Two: The Suspects

i: *The Highest in the Land*

The most astonishing of all suspects' names was put forward as recently as 1970: the Duke of Clarence, Queen Victoria's grandson and heir to the throne of England. This sensational suggestion received wide publicity and upset many people. It was published in 1970 under the title 'A Solution?' in the reputable magazine the *Criminologist* and it was written by a surgeon, Thomas Stowell CBE, MD, FRCS.

Stowell was scrupulous in referring to his suspect as 'S', but so careless – or careful – in dropping clues that the identity was unmistakable. His protest, 'I would never dream of doing harm to a family whom I love and admire by revealing the name,' was disingenuous. So was his reply when Kenneth Allsop pressed him on television in '24 Hours' on 2 November 1970: 'I have no comment to make on that, sir.' Allsop continued: 'I confess that I don't altogether understand your reluctance, because if you didn't want to identify the person as being the Duke of Clarence why did you go all the way round the subject filling in so many details which are really rather easily tracked down?' A reasonable question, but Stowell deflected it as usual : 'Yes,' he said, 'I'm content to leave it at that. I have such regard for the family and personally owe members of the family so much myself, that I refrain, I am averse, strongly averse, to causing them any embarrassment.' If that was really his intention, Stowell failed lamentably. Having kept his theory private for so many years, it is surprising that he allowed it to be published at all. But Stowell was then in his eighties and died shortly after the revelation. Perhaps old age confused his judgement.

After his death, his son was apparently so upset by the scandal that he destroyed all the relevant papers, making it harder than ever to assess the theory. One of the few people whom Stowell had confided in was Colin Wilson, who has given me access to his own notes. He met Stowell for the first time in 1960. 'He was in his early seventies then; a friendly, likeable man. He told me he was still practising surgery – although, noting the way his hand shook as he cut his steak, I wondered how much longer that could go on.'

In the *Criminologist*, Stowell maintained his absurd mystery about the identity of his suspect, calling him 'S': 'He was the heir to power and wealth. His family, for fifty years, had earned the love and admiration of large numbers of people by its devotion to public service to all classes, particularly the poor, but as well to industry and the workers. His grandmother, who outlived him, was very much the stern Victorian matriarch, widely and deeply respected. His father, to whose title he was heir, was a gay cosmopolitan and did much to improve the status of England internationally. His mother was an unusually beautiful woman with a gracious personal charm, and was greatly beloved to all who knew her.'

He told Colin Wilson that he was convinced that Jack the Ripper was the Duke of Clarence. Stowell was under the impression that Wilson had reached such a conclusion himself, from written comments suggesting that the Ripper was 'a gentleman', 'young', with a 'blond moustache'. Wilson explained that he'd found all these details in the reports of *The Times* during the murders, as Stowell should have realised.

Stowell claimed he had seen the private papers of the late Sir William Gull, physician to Guy's Hospital and Physician in Ordinary to the Royal Family. When Gull died his daughter asked Stowell to examine his papers, as she believed they contained information that was highly confidential. They did indeed, claiming that the Duke of Clarence had not in fact died in 1892 but was kept in a mental home near Sandringham with 'softening of the brain' due to syphilis.

In the *Criminologist*, Stowell outlined the background and explanation for this tragic climax. 'After the education traditional for an English aristocrat, at the age of sixteen "S" went on a cruise round the world with a number of high-spirited boys of approximately his age group. He was, perhaps, too popular and gregarious for his own safety. It is recorded that he went to many gay parties ashore.' The cruise referred to was a three-year tour of the world with his younger brother, later King George V, on HMS *Bacchante*, and the 'high-spirited boys' were sailors, one of whom, according to Stowell, seduced the Duke and gave him the syphilis that killed him at the age of twenty-eight. 'I think he was seduced in Australia or before his arrival there,' Stowell wrote to Wilson but there seems a confusion of fact, for in the *Criminologist* he writes of 'S': 'I believe that at one of the many shore parties which he enjoyed in the West Indies on his world journey be became infected with syphilis. Some six weeks later he had an important public appointment in what was then one of our Colonies. At the last moment he cancelled that appointment on account of "a trifling ailment". The abandonment of an important engagement on account of a trifling ailment is unusual unless it is causing severe pain or obvious disfigurement, e.g. toothache or the development of a visible rash.'

'This "trifling ailment" may well have been the appearance of the skin rash of secondary syphilis appearing six weeks after the primary infection acquired in the West Indies.'

On his return to England before his nineteenth birthday, Clarence became a man-about-town and was known affectionately 'to the working classes' as 'Collars and Cuffs' because of the extravagance of his clothes. Stowell refers to a photograph of 'S', dressed immaculately on the bank of a river holding a fishing-rod: 'He is wearing a four inch to four and half inch stiff starched collar and is showing two inches of shirt-cuff at each wrist.' (See illustration no. 15.)

He entered the army at the age of twenty-one and resigned his commission when he was twenty-four. Stowell claims that this was after a raid on a male-brothel in Cleveland Street off the Tottenham Court Road which was kept by a man called Hammond and frequented by homosexual aristocrats. A newspaper revealed that, 'Among those arrested was the highest in the land'. Stowell mentioned this press cutting to Wilson on a number of occasions and referred to another item about telegraph boys receiving presents of gold pencils.

The Duke was disposed of by sending him on another cruise; and, according to Stowell, it was after this return that his brain gave way and he started the murders. Throughout this time he was under the care of Sir William Gull: 'It was said that on more than one occasion Sir William Gull was seen in the neighbourhood of Whitechapel on the night of a murder. It would not surprise me to know,' wrote Stowell, 'that he was there for the purpose of certifying the murderer to be insane so that he might be put under restraint as were other lunatics apprehended in connection with the murders.' At some point the Royal Family were told the 'truth' and the Duke was interned in a mental home. Stowell even believed that he had been caught after the murder of Eddowes but escaped five weeks later to murder Kelly.

What is the basis for these extraordinary claims? Stowell produces the old story of a spiritualist called R. J. Lees whose 'uncanny gifts' were used by the police and even by Queen Victoria who invited him twice to the Palace – or so it is claimed. (I have been told that Lees recommended John Brown as a medium.) By a coincidence, this story was actually told to Colin Wilson's first wife by Lees's daughter Eva, so he already knew it first-hand: 'The story goes that Lees had several vivid dreams of the murders before they happened, and in his dreams he saw the face of the murderer. One day, travelling on a bus along Bayswater Road, he recognised the murderer sitting opposite him – a respectable-looking man with a frock coat and top hat. When the man got off the bus, so did Lees – and followed him to a house in Park Lane.

'It turned out to be the house of a famous physician, with connections with the royal family. When Lees went to the police with his story, their first reaction was incredulity; but they checked with the surgeon's wife, and she admitted that her husband had been behaving very oddly recently, and that she was afraid he was going insane.

'The police kept a watch on the doctor, and actually caught him in the act of leaving the house with his carving knife in a black bag. He was interned in a mental home for the rest of his life.'

It is claimed that a bogus funeral took place with a coffin weighted with stones and his family in mourning. The story of Lees is repeated at length in *Ghost Detectives* by Fred Archer.

Stowell uses this theory to support his accusation: 'It interests me to speculate [a devastating phrase!] whether the 'imposing mansion' to which Lees led the police was 74 Brook Street, Grosvenor Square, the home of Sir William Gull, and whether Mr Archer's story is a variation of one told me by Sir William Gull's daughter, Caroline. She was the wife of Theodore Dyke Acland, MD, FRCP, one time my beloved Chief. I knew them both intimately and often enjoyed the hospitality of their home in Bryanston Square, over many years.

'Mrs Acland's story was that at the time of the Ripper murders, her mother, Lady Gull, was greatly annoyed one night by an unappointed visit from a police officer, accompanied by a man who called himself a 'medium' and she was irritated by their impudence in asking her a number of questions which seemed to her impertinent. She answered their questions with non-committal replies such as 'I do not know', 'I cannot tell you that', 'I am afraid I cannot answer that question'.

'Later Sir William himself came down and in answer to the questions said he occasionally suffered from "lapses of memory since he had a slight stroke in 1887"; he said that he once had discovered blood on his shirt. This is not surprising, if he had medically examined the Ripper after one of the murders.'

I should have thought this highly surprising. A more rational explanation, though still far-fetched, was given by Stowell to Colin Wilson: that some of the signs pointing to Gull's guilt, like the blood on his shirt, were deliberately designed to divert suspicion. In other words, Gull had nobly offered himself as a decoy. However, the whole theory concerning Gull falls to bits when one learns that the 'slight stroke' was in fact a paralytic stroke which resulted in his complete withdrawal from practise in 1887, including attendance on the Royal Family.

As further evidence, Stowell laid great emphasis on the physical resemblance of the Duke of Clarence to eye-witness reports of 'medium height' (a worthless description) and more particularly of a fair moustache and a deer-stalker hat. This hat struck Stowell as possessing a symbolic importance: 'With his father's friends he stalked deer on the family estate in Scotland. This gave him many opportunities of watching the dressing of the carcasses, and if he wished, of assisting in the operation. In doing this he would have learned how to remove bowels, kidney, liver, heart, lungs and uterus neatly.

'The sex instinct of the psychopath is sometimes stimulated watching dissections or mutilations. This happened to the Ripper. When later, his mind was broken down still further by the poison of the syphilitic infection, it became directed towards his crimes.

'It is significant to remember that Jack the Ripper wore the deer-stalker's hat, as a kind of ritual vestment, when he murdered and mutilated the Spitalfields prostitutes.'

Believing in his theory so strongly, Stowell was able to use facts to his advantage. He admitted that under the skilful medical supervision of Gull, and after a further cruise, the Duke of Clarence improved sufficiently to take part in public life on at least three occasions. 'On each of these occasions, important though they were, he made speeches but each speech contained little more than a hundred words. This indicates that he had lost much of his former ebullience and that he was on the downward path from the manic stage of syphilis to the depression and dementia which in time must inevitably overtake him.' He concluded: '... he relapsed and died of bronchopneumonia a few years later – the usual cause of death in such cases.'

This implies that the Royal Family connived at a charade at his death following a 'flu-epidemic in January 1892, 'when the Queen put Windsor Castle at the disposal of the Prince of Wales and his Household, on the occasion of the funeral of Prince Albert Victor, Duke of Clarence,' as recorded by Arthur Ponsonby.

After Stowell appeared on the television programme '24 Hours', and the story was repeated in the *Sunday Times* mentioning the Duke of Clarence by name, a number of people protested that he could not have committed the murders as he was in Scotland on 29 and 30 September, when Catherine Eddowes was killed. Though he might have escaped for the night, it seems that Clarence was at Sandringham from 3 to 12 November, and consequently not in London on the 9th when Mary Kelly was murdered. The 9th was also his father's birthday. After the 12th, Clarence went to Copenhagen to represent his father at the Danish King's accession to the throne.

It is such discrepancies *after* the murders that make the Clarence theory so implausible.

The possibility that the Royal Family did not know the full extent of the Duke's condition is refuted by Stowell's statement that Gull 'Informed —— that his son was dying of syphilis of the brain in 1889'. Medical opinion does not support Stowell's theory, on the basis that a general paralysis of the insane due to syphilis, takes longer to develop.

Admittedly, the Duke of Clarence remains an enigma. It is difficult to prove Stowell's charges fraudulent because this would entail a statement from the Royal Family, which is 'not done'. However, the Royal Family have let it be known that they regarded the charges as ridiculous.

Neither Colin Wilson nor I ever believed the story, which is only intriguing speculation. Judging by Colin Wilson's remarks, Stowell had an almost schoolboyish glee in his theory and it became the harmless obsession of an old man – until he suddenly allowed it to be published. It is a sad irony that he died only a few days later, as if in giving away his 'secret' he had given away part of his life.

In June 1972, the Duke of Clarence theory was aired again, in 'The Other Victorians' on BBC Radio 4, and later in the biography of the Duke by Michael Harrison. I learnt of Michael Harrison's theory when I took part in a television discussion (for Westward TV's 'Format') chaired by Colin Wilson, at the end of March. Harrison revealed that his suspect was not the Duke of Clarence but his friend (and lover?) James Stephen. Born in 1859, Stephen was the son of Sir James Fitzjames Stephen, a judge of the High Court from 1879 to 1891. His uncle was Leslie Stephen, the father of Vanessa Bell and Virginia Woolf.

When he was a boy, James saw little of his father who was in India acting as legal counsellor to the Viceroy. He won a scholarship to Eton in 1871, rowed in the college boats and excelled at the Eton wall game. In 1878 he went to King's College, Cambridge and was elected President of the Union in 1882. He appeared in a Greek play for which 'his massive frame and generally noble appearance fitted him admirably'. He was called to the Bar, and contributed to magazines, but on 29 December 1886, at Felixstowe, he had 'an accident, the effects of which were far more serious than appeared at the time; he was watching an engine employed in pumping water when he received a terrible blow on the head.'

In June 1888, probably due to his father's influence, he was appointed to the clerkship of assize on the South Wales Circuit. This hardly suggests that he was suddenly to turn to murder, but it is now that Leslie Stephen raises a suspicion: 'Clearer symptoms showed themselves before long of the disease caused by the accident. I have no wish to dwell upon that painful topic... it gradually became manifest that he was suffering from a terrible disease. He had painful periods of excitement and depression. Eccentricities of behaviour caused growing anxiety to his family.'

Yet in 1890 and 1891, he spoke at the Cambridge Union and published two volumes of verse. He died on 3 February 1892.

Michael Harrison makes many fascinating suggestions in his new book *Clarence*. He claims there were ten Ripper murders altogether, linking this theory to the rhyme (from the ballad *Kaphoozelum*):

> For though he paid his women well
> This syphilitic spawn of hell,
> Struck down each year and tolled the bell
> For ten Harlots of Jerusalem.

And he claims further that these ten murders occurred on Royal anniversaries as a sort of 'blood-sacrifice'. Referring to Kelly's murder on Lord Mayor's Day, Harrison says the date was chosen as: 'a "birthday present" for the Prince of Wales, father of that Eddy whose "jilting" of Stephen had finally turned a brain already ripe for post-traumatic mania.'

Harrison quotes several remarkable poems by Stephen to prove his pathological dislike of women, such as this contribution to *Granta* in 1891, 'A Thought':

> If all the harm that women have done
> Were put in a bundle and rolled into one,
> Earth would not hold it.

Less convincingly, Harrison traces parallels between Stephen's poems and those allegedly sent by the Ripper, claiming that the phrase 'Box of Toys' (in a letter to Mr Lusk) was rhyming slang of the day for 'boys' and familiar to 'toffs' like Stephen.

There are two gigantic flaws in his brilliant but récherché theory: the claim that there were ten murders, for which there is no justification; and the basic assertion that Stowell's suspect 'S' did not refer to Clarence at all. Correctly, he points out that a number of dates and details – on the tour of HMS *Bacchante*, for example – do not tally with Clarence, but surely this is Stowell's carelessness. There can be no doubt that Stowell meant them to apply to Clarence; his detailed description of 'S' by the river bank, fishing rod in hand (reproduced as illustration no. 15), proves that beyond doubt.

I asked Michael Harrison why – if Stephen was the Ripper – no one had ever heard of this before. He replied that it had been 'hushed up'. But such a scandal would be difficult to conceal absolutely, and it is surprising that no word of it ever reached Sir Melville Macnaghten, for example.

ii: 'Jill the Ripper'

Though it might not seem so at first sight, the theory that Jack the Ripper was a woman is more plausible. If she had been a midwife, as William Stewart suggested (*Jack the Ripper: A new theory*) this would have removed her from suspicion. Her voluminous clothes would have hidden the blood-stains; she could have carried her tools in a bag; she would have had a rough anatomical knowledge; and always the perfect alibi for being out in the streets at night. If she had worked in the district, she would have known those streets intimately. William Stewart even suggests a motive: that 'Jill the Ripper' was a midwife-abortionist who had been exposed to the police by a prostitute and sent to prison. Now she was released and taking her revenge.

The theory appears to fit the case of Kelly. She was pregnant and might have admitted a midwife in the early hours of the morning. Then there was the curious evidence of witnesses who saw Kelly after her death. The explanation here is simple: that the murderess was covered in blood and burnt her clothes in the fire, accounting for the melted kettle and the charred remains which contained traces of velvet and a bonnet. Then she dressed in Kelly's clothes and left Miller's Court at dawn. This sounds convincing; but Kelly's own clothes were found at the foot of the bed and no others were missing. Also, an overcoat was hanging by the window which would have been a natural covering. Colin Wilson believes that the Ripper was naked as he mutilated the body by the light from the fire. Also, it seems unlikely that Kelly would have admitted a midwife on a night when she was known to be penniless and was trying to pick up men. But it is in relation to the other victims that the theory falls to pieces. Why should these women have accompanied a midwife into the backyards of Whitechapel? There is no convincing reason. It has been suggested that when Mary Nicholls boasted her bonnet, it had been given to her by a woman because she would have mentioned any present

72

from a man. An interesting pyschological observation, but equally she could have earned the money from a man and bought it herself.

There is no reason why such a murderer should not have been a woman. It has been known in similar cases. Within two weeks of the murder, known in America as 'The Black Dahlia', Captain Donohue suspected a woman for a number of reasons, as recorded by David Rowan in *Famous American Crimes*. 'The nature of the injuries,' according to Rowan, 'the peculiarly vicious spite with which they had been inflicted – pointed to the deadlier of the species ... In certain details,' he continues, 'there is a marked similarity between the Dahlia murder, and the unsolved sex killings which followed it, and the notorious "Jack the Ripper" killings in London towards the end of the last century.'

But despite that, and the general plausibility of the idea, we must conclude that there is no positive evidence whatever.

iii: *The Satanic Dr Stanley*

Most murderers have a specific motive. The apparent lack of motive is one explanation for the panic in 1888, when murder for 'mere' sexual gratification was less easily understood. In his book on Jack the Ripper published in 1929, Leonard Matters asked the vital question, Why did he commit the murders?' and gave the answer. Archibald Forbes, a war correspondent, had already suggested that 'his lunacy is the lunacy of revenge, possibly complicated by physical disease, clearly he is a man not unaccustomed in the manner of accosting these poor women as they are wont to be accosted. Possibly a dissolute man, he fell a victim of a specific contagion, and so seriously that in the sequel he lost his career. It is a curious fact that some men are so constituted as to conceive and foster a conviction of bitter hate against the hopeless creature involved.'

Though he was too reticent to use the word 'syphilis', Matters took this Theory further in stating that the Ripper was searching for one prostitute in particular: 'This woman he knew definitely to be resident in the East End of London. There was no need to search elsewhere for her, and hence no reason for him to change the locale of his nightly operations, given his determination to find and kill that woman, no matter how great was the risk to his own liberty and life. Mary Kelly was that woman, and when he had killed her he was satisfied. His motive was the direct one of personal vengeance upon that woman, and when she was dead at his hands he was content.'

There is one piece of evidence that supports such a theory: the curious coincidence that Catherine Eddowes was also known as 'Kate Kelly', as if the murderer was searching for a woman with that name. For the woman was not known to him by sight; according to Matters it was not the murderer who had caught the disease, but his son.

Leonard Matters, was determined that his theory was right: 'Only by accepting the existence of Dr Stanley, the surgeon – the lonely, silent, satanic Dr Stanley is it possible to delineate what must have been the nature of "Jack the Ripper".' But this sweeping statement is followed by the admission: 'That such a man of such a character and such a life story did really exist in 1888 it is beyond my hope to prove.' Even so, one expects more than the assurance that it is 'definitely based on the recital of an anonymous surgeon in Buenos Aires'.

It is this surgeon who starts the story in his own words, recalling the time when he was a medical student in a London hospital where the brilliant Dr Stanley was an honorary surgeon. Since the early death of his wife, probably from cancer, the doctor had withdrawn inside himself and to the outside world he seemed aloof and embittered. The student glimpsed the human side of his nature, all the pride and love which was lavished on his only child – Herbert. Dr Stanley felt sufficiently at ease with the student to show him his museum of surgical specimens, collected in his search for a cure for cancer: 'Here is the patient work of a lifetime! All I regret is that a man's own life is so short. I can never live long enough to complete what I set out to do, but my boy will do it. My son will be famous. He will be hailed as a saviour of humanity.'

The student saw 'The touch of a master hand', 'the audacious use of the knife', but then the doctor revealed another side of his character when he attacked his colleagues, including Lister, as 'hacker': 'Any butcher is, in my opinion, superior to them ... I would like to have them under me for a while just to teach them something of the fine art of surgery.'

'He said this with so much vehemence,' recalled the student later, 'that I looked at him. The calm man of science had disappeared. In his eyes there was a strange brilliance. He was nervous and agitated, and gave me the impression of a neurotic obsessed by an idea that he was carrying on a fight with invisible enemies who dared to dispute with him the possession of a skill that he alone might claim. Perhaps he was not concerned for himself, but his whole manner and outlook suggested to me that he was engaged in his own mind in a desperate battle for the future of his son. There was no doubt Dr Stanley had centred all his hopes on that boy, and, looking at his museum, he saw in it not only the proof that he was right in his theory and surgical methods, but that his son's future was wrapped up in his own victory over those he imagined to be his enemies. Perhaps he was mad.'

On his way home, he wonders what would happen if some disaster overtook the son. 'I could not help thinking that a tragedy like that would drive Dr Stanley to the verge of desperation. If anything happened to let loose the rancour against the world, then slumbering in the bosom of this strange man, the consequences would be awful. Terrible!'

75

Leonard Matters, without changing a syllable of style, took up the story: 'The tragedy happened.' Not surprisingly, Herbert Stanley was 'handsome, elegant, distinguished ... destined under the eye of his father to fortune and fame,' but he was also destined to die 'a hopeless wreck for whom medical skill had, at that time, no sure aid to offer'.

Herbert first saw Mary Kelly on the rowdy Boat Race night of 1886, their eyes met and they went off to Paris to live happily 'till he had known the truth. Then he had struck her in his madness and had finished with her for ever.' Several weeks later, his father 'took the news as a strong man takes a blow'.

Together they tried to fight the disease which travelled through the boy's blood. Though Dr Stanley could have performed miracles with the knife, he was powerless in such a case and had to call in physicians who were equally helpless. One night he asked his son for the name of the woman: 'Young Stanley's eyes blazed. Father and soon understood one another.' When his son died 'the father gazed for the last time on the distorted features of his dead boy, not a muscle of his mask-like face moved. No sign of sorrow did he show. The boy had gone. It was well.

'At that thought Dr Stanley raised his eyes from the face that he had loved so proudly and so deeply. In a voice that scarcely rose above a whisper he said: "I will find the woman. When I find her, I will kill her; by God I will!"'

His hunt began in the West End. By now he hated all prostitutes, but he confided in a girl of seventeen who told Leonard Matters her part in the story sixty years later when she was called Mrs North. Discovering that Kelly had taken to drink and descended to the depths of the East End, he adopted the disguise of a labourer so that 'slumdom' would not be alerted by the questions of a mysterious stranger.

His first victim was Martha Turner: 'Dr Stanley asked the woman whom she knew among those of her kind. She named

76

them all. Then he plied her with direct questions. The woman did not know Mary – had never heard of her. In the darkness a sinewy hand shot out and closed about the neck of Martha Turner. No cry escaped from her lips. No struggle was possible, for as she sank unconscious to the floor the knife was at her throat.'

When he finally tracked Kelly down, he was appalled: 'This was the girl who had attracted his son – the drink-sodden drab! Was it worth while killing her, when she had doomed herself?'

But he did kill her, as he had vowed, and left for South America. His former student gasps with surprise, as well he might, when he receives a letter delivered to him by hand: 'His old master in Buenos Aires! How strange!'

Dear Sir, At the request of a patient who says you will remember him as Dr Stanley, I write to inform you that he is lying in this hospital in a dangerous condition. He is suffering from cancer, and though an operation has been performed successfully, complications have arisen which make the end inevitable. Dr Stanley would like to see you . . . Jose Riché, Senior House Surgeon.

The student hurried to the hospital. 'There a dying man turned his face and smiled in welcome. Almost vain was the effort to discern in that pain-racked face the stern and immobile features of the one-time Dr Stanley – the brilliant London surgeon, so strong, so purposeful. It was another face that fixed a tragic glance upon the visitor. "I am Dr Stanley.'" When his former student 'sought to embrace' him, Dr. Stanley pushed his arms away and made his death-bed confession:

'No, no! don't touch me yet. No decent man should come near me . . . Before I leave this world I must clear my conscience . . . Nobody but you must hear what I say.' The dark eyes of Dr Stanley glowed upon his visitor.

'Have you ever heard of "Jack the Ripper"?' he whispered hoarsely.

'Yes.'

'Well – I am he!'

'You!' In horror the other man shrank back. 'Yes I'. Within a few moments Dr Stanley fell back dead.

The theory of 'Dr Stanley' is intriguing because it does present a genuine motive. There is the coincidence of Eddowes being known as 'Kate Kelly', suggesting that the murders stopped because he found the woman he was looking for in Mary Kelly. It is possible, even, to draw conclusions from the mutilations of his earlier victims, as if the murderer was searching for the foetus he found inside Mary Kelly: his own child? But as for the motive of revenge, it was stated by the doctors that Mary Kelly did not have any venereal disease. Also, as Donald McCormick points out, though there was no positive cure for syphilis at that time, there was treatment and it is unlikely that Dr Stanley's son would have died in such a short space of time.

In answer to my appeal on television I received a letter that does not name Dr Stanley but does support such a theory. Mr Barca of Streatham spent the years 1910–20 in Buenos Aires, where he was told of a certain bar called 'Sally's Bar', 'frequented by sailors and people of ill-repute'. He was told that it was owned by Jack the Ripper and that Sally was a young girl he had brought over with him in 1889. After making enough money, Sally returned to Europe and settled in Paris.

Leonard Matters made the bold claim that 'the only fictitious thing about the story of Dr Stanley is his name'. I believe that this part of his book is entirely a work of fiction, including his meeting in the Café Monico with Mrs North sixty years later (surely he meant forty years later?) I suspect that Matters began the story of 'Dr Stanley' as a novel, unexceptionable as such but unacceptable in the context of a documentary.

iv: *The Jewish Slaughterman*

In *Jack the Ripper, In Fact and Fiction,* Robin Odell examines and dismisses various suspects, and comes up with one of his own. It has some plausibility if one remembers the conditions of the East End at the time, swamped with people of different nationalities and religions. The excuse was made for Sir Charles Warren that he wiped out the message on the wall – 'The Jewes are not the men to be blamed for nothing' – in order to avoid an outburst of anti-semitism. But the astonishing thing was the lack of anti-semitism, in spite of letters to the newspapers suggesting that a Jew was responsible and the short-lived scare of Pizer. That the Jewish population of Whitechapel did not become a scapegoat is a tribute both to the commonsense of the cockney and to the impeccable behaviour of the Jews themselves.

Robin Odell suggests that a slaughterman, steeped in Old Testament law, might have felt a religious justification in murdering such women. Slaughtermen were a common sight in 1888; Odell refers to the Jewish *abattoir* in Aldgate High Street which 'bustled with preparations for the ritual act of slaughter which formed such an essential part of Jewish life. Jews were forbidden to eat of meat that had not been properly slaughtered according to ancient law and custom. The increases in the East End Jewish population in the early 1880s caused a rising demand for properly prepared kosher meat.'

Odell pointed out, that in the early hours of the morning, even with bloodstains, a slaughterman would not have looked suspicious. The Jewish ritual of slaughter, in which the meat was drained of blood, was known as *shechita,* and the elite of the slaughtermen were called *shochets,* 'concerning whose anatomical knowledge and expertise with the knife there are no doubts at all'.

'*Abattoir* assistants,' wrote Odell, 'prepared the animal for the ritual by hobbling its legs with rope and "casting" its throat in position for the knife. The ritual slaughterman took from its case the long steel knife which he had spent many hours grinding and honing. This was the ceremonial knife which he would use to kill the animal that lay before him.'

This knife was razor-sharp, without the slightest blemish. The slaughter had to be perfect, for the meat to be eaten. When it had been tested, the *shochet* drew it across the animal's throat: 'A quick forward and backward stroke, and the work was done: the throat was cut through to the bone. Death was immediate, and as the *shochet* stepped back the animal's life-blood gushed to the ground from the severed arteries and veins.'

After the killing he first of all has to make sure that the wind-pipe and gullet are properly cut through, then he makes a sort of post-mortem in which he examines the lungs, heart and then the stomach, intestines, liver, kidneys, etc., for any sign of disease. Even the fat lying upon the kidneys was 'carefully removed with a special knife kept for the purpose, as Jews were forbidden to eat the fat of a slaughtered animal.'

This could explain the mutilations by the Ripper, but hardly the conspicuous lack of blood around the victims. Referring to a lack of blood on the Ripper's clothes, Odell makes a comparison with Japanese executions: 'When decapitation was performed, the executioner followed the killing stroke of the sword with a kick which sent the body toppling away from him. In this way he was able to avoid the discomfort of being spattered with blood. No doubt slaughterers employed similar methods and for the same reasons.' But if so, there would surely have been even more blood on the ground?

'There can be no question but that a slaughterman, and particularly a *shochet*, would have possessed in every detail the medical skills attributed to Jack the Ripper.' This is more reasonable than the assertion that the *shochet* would have inspired an immediate trust from his victim because of his special religious status. '*Shochets* were ordained priests because their profession was primarily a religious one, and, being minor clerics, many of them carried the title of reverend.' Certainly this might apply to the victims if they had been Jewish, but why these prostitutes, why prostitutes at all? Odell gives the answer: 'Sexual psychopaths in some instances attribute their hideous deeds to the commands of God. They say this genuinely, and not as a ploy seeking sympathy for what they have done. In most cases there is no remorse, for they feel that their acts have been justified.'

It is now that Odell supplies a necessary motive: 'This is one example of a type of religious delusion that afflicts some psychopaths, and a theory along these lines might be applied to the Ripper murders. A ritual slaughterman steeped in Old Testament law might have felt some religious justification for killing prostitutes. Talmudic law was harsh where harlotry was concerned, and in certain cases whores could be punished by strangulation or stoning.' This last point is significant, as it seems likely that the Ripper did strangle his victims, as well as cutting their throats.

As for the mentality which enabled the Ripper to continue with such cool confidence, Odell claims that 'Remorse was an alien feeling to the Ripper, for his mind was filled with an overpowering appetite that only death could end. In his twisted way he could claim too a sense of religious justification in clearing the East End streets of harlots. In such ways do wretched prostitutes become the butt of the sexual psychopath's inadequacy. *Incapable of normal sexual relations* [my italics, for this is a most significant point], and inferior to the task of seduction, these perverts often seek the easy acceptance of prostitutes, and then in a cruel travesty of morals claim justification for killing them.' There is much sense in this last sentence, but I am unconvinced by the blunt assertion, 'Of all the likely murderers in London in 1888 the *shochet* alone possessed all the qualities of motive, method and opportunity to murder prostitutes in the East End.'

In support of his theory, Odell quotes Sir Robert Anderson, who succeeded Warren as Commissioner, from his book: *The Lighter Side of My Official Life*. Anderson claims as a 'definitely ascertained fact' that the Ripper and his people were certain low-class Polish Jews and that people of the class in

81

the East End would not give up one of their number to Gentile justice. Odell admits that this last accusation is unfair. He is honest enough to conclude: 'The Whitechapel murderer is unique because of his anonymity, and all attempts to unravel his identity inevitably fall short of absolute verification.' He adds: 'Nevertheless people will continue to seek solutions to mysteries, and very often the simplest construction on what is known is the one that will have an eventual claim to reality.'

v: *The Lodger*

Alfred Hitchcock's first film was *The Lodger*, sub-titled 'A Story of the London Fog', made in 1926. It tells the familiar story of a kindly landlady who begins to suspect that her handsome young lodger is none other than 'The Avenger', a sex-maniac with a fancy for gold-curled girls, who is terrorising London. After a mob has almost lynched him, it turns out that he was searching for the man who murdered his sister.

A variation on the theme was told to me by Sacheverell Sitwell. He and his brother Osbert – who repeated it in *Noble Essences* – heard the story from the painter Walter Sickert. Some years after the Ripper murders, Sickert rented a room in a London suburb run by an old couple. He used to talk to the landlady as she dusted around him, and one day she asked him if he knew who had occupied the room before. When Sickert said 'No' she paused, and replied 'Jack the Ripper!' Apparently he had been a delicate-looking veterinary student suffering from consumption, and after he had been there a month or two he took to staying out all night. Then the couple heard him coming in again around six in the morning and walk up and down his room until the first editions of the morning papers were on sale when he'd creep downstairs and go to the corner to buy one. Later the old man noticed traces of cloth in the fireplace, as if the lodger had burnt the suit he had been wearing the night before. The couple also noticed that though everyone was talking about the series of murders, the lodger never mentioned them. He seemed to know no one, and talked to no one. 'The old couple did not know what to make of the matter,' recorded Osbert Sitwell. 'Week by week his health grew worse, and it seemed improbable that this gentle, ailing, silent youth should be responsible for such crimes. They could hardly credit their own senses – and then, before they could make up their minds whether to warn the police or not, the lodger's health had suddenly failed alarmingly, and his mother – a widow who was devoted to him – had come to fetch him back to Bournemouth, where she lived. From that moment the murders stopped. He died three months later.'

Sacheverell Sitwell added the postscript that Sickert had scribbled the name of the lodger in the book he was reading at the time, a French edition of Casanova's *Memoirs*, and that he had given this book to a friend afterwards. The Sitwells traced the friend, only to learn that the book – with the Ripper's 'name' in the margin – had been destroyed in the Blitz.

I include this as a highly entertaining tale, but feel that it can be dismissed as just that.

vi: *The Tsarist Secret Agent*

Robin Odell's book has the sub-title 'In Fact and Fiction'. It is easy to see how inseparable these have become over the years. In presenting such careful research as Odell's, I have tried to keep to the original words of the salient points. With Donald McCormick's *The Identity of Jack the Ripper*, I recommend you to read the entire book.

McCormick leans towards fiction himself in his supposition of detail. This is a dangerous trap, as all those who have written biographies discover. McCormick falls straight into it. He records a conversation between two soldiers in the 'Two Brewers' on the night that Martha Turner was murdered:

'I'm fed up to the bloomin' teeth wiv these gels. Not time for anyone but a matelot. Let's go somewhere else.'

'Wot baht cuttin' back on our tracks and going to the City Road. We could pop in the Eagle and 'ave one and then go an' see this rorty gel wot sings "My Soldier Laddie".'

Apparently the soldier was referring to 'that Bella Delmere' and his mate tells him that she calls herself Marie Lloyd now.

I chose this passage partly because it referred to Marie Lloyd in whom I had a special interest, but also as a good example of supposition. Apparently I was wrong; in the revised edition of his book, Donald McCormick claims: 'Thus the conversation of the soldiers in the first chapter are taken from statements made to the police and are not a fictional trick thought up by the author.' I stand corrected and surprised. Incidentally, the soldiers were rather out of date for it was nearly three years since Marie appeared as Bella Delmere and that had been for a few weeks only. But it shows that the borderline between fact and fiction is remarkably thin. As for later details – 'a drunken laugh from Martha and a blush of embarrassment from the young soldier' – surely these must be supposition? But even so, this does not diminish the mammoth and meticulous research that McCormick has undertaken.

At the same time, his conclusions are so intricate and confusing that I doubt if I can do them justice even though I have checked with the resumé by Odell. This is why I advise reading the book as a whole. McCormick returns to the theory of the Pole or Russian suspect and produces the most interesting evidence so far. He accuses a man called Pedachenko – but it is not as simple as that. In support of his theory, he quotes a criminologist called Dr Dutton who was a friend of Chief Inspector Abberline who led the team of CID officers in their search for the Ripper. On the curious basis that English visitors to the East End were not as well dressed as the Ripper was supposed to be, Dutton urged the Inspector to look out for Poles and Russians: 'They could pass for Englishmen at a pinch, providing no one heard them speak. They are fundamentally barbarous, treat women with scant respect, tend to have a brutal nature, sexually speaking. And you will find a larger number of Poles and Russians with a smattering of surgery and a knowledge of anatomy than in almost any other race.'

These assertions may have seemed less grotesque then than now. Among the mass of immigrants, a number of East European anarchists had settled in Whitechapel and formed their own societies in clubs like the one off Berners Street, behind which Elizabeth Stride was murdered. Unlike in other countries, they were able to live in England without persecution or even interference by the police. Inspector Abberline looked for the murderer among such men. The detective work involves a collection of names, compared in its complexity by Odell to a Russian telephone directory. In a barber's shop in Whitechapel, Abberline heard an assistant being called by the name of 'Ludwig', who bore a surprising resemblance to a German of the same name who had been arrested as a Ripper suspect, and released. Discovering from his files that this was a different 'Ludwig', Abberline returned to the barber's shop to find the assistant had gone, that his real name was really 'Schloski', or something like that, and he was Polish. Finally, Abberline traced the man to another barber's in Tottenham and discovered that his real name was Severin Antoniovich Klosowski, who became known to the police many years later as the poisoner George Chapman.

Klosowski had been a *feldscher* in the Russian army. A *feldscher* was an unqualified doctor's assistant and the point is made that many barbers in the East End at that time employed *feldschers* for minor surgical work, like removing moles and warts. Klosowski had just arrived in England and Abberline was so suspicious that when Klosowski, or Chapman as he had become, was arrested for murder in 1903 he declared: 'I see you have caught the Ripper at last,' or words to that effect. Dr Dutton claims that Abberline realised he might have been mistaken when he discovered that 'the Polish barber-surgeon had a double in London. This double was a Russian and also a *feldscher* and sometimes posed as Klosowski, confusing the picture still further. Donald McCormick says this double was Dr Alexander Pedachenko.

Another source quoted is William Le Queux who had been a secret agent in the First War. In his book *Things I Know About Kings, Celebrities and Crooks* Le Queux revealed: 'the Kerensky Government handed to me, in confidence, a great quantity of documents which had been found in the safe of Rasputin's house in order that I might write an account of the scoundrel's amazing career.' Among these documents, intended to discredit Rasputin, was a manuscript in French – allegedly written by Rasputin himself – called 'Great Russian Criminals'. This claimed that the Ripper had been identified as Pedachenko by a member of the Anarchist Centre in the East End of London by a man called Nideroest. Le Queux quoted this key passage:

The reports of Nideroest's discovery amused our secret police greatly, for, as a matter of fact, they knew the whole details at the time, and had themselves actively aided and encouraged the crimes, in order to exhibit to the world certain defects of the English police system, there having been some misunderstanding and rivalry between our police and the British. It was, indeed, for that reason that Pedachenko, the greatest and boldest of all Russian lunatics was encouraged to go to London and commit that series of atrocious crimes, in which our agents of police aided him. Eventually, at the orders of the Ministry of the Interior the Secret Police smuggled the assassin out of London, and, as Count Luiskovo, he landed at Ostend, and was conducted by a secret agent to Moscow. While there he was, a few months later, caught red-handed attempting to murder and mutilate a woman named Vogak and was eventually sent to an asylum where he died in 1908.

After the return to Russia of Levitski and the woman,

Winberg, (two accomplices) the Secret Police deemed it wise to suppress them, and they were therefore exiled to Yakutsk. Such are the actual facts of 'Jack the Ripper Mystery', which still puzzled the whole world.

McCormick concedes that this is 'a fantastic story', though he appears to accept it. He goes on to quote Dr Dutton: 'It is a great pity that he [Le Queux] did not follow up what is a useful clue. By failing to do so, and by taking the Rasputin Ms at its face value, he has only made a fool of himself. Further examination might have shown that Pedachenko was Klosowski's double. The fact that Pedachenko was a doctor at a Russian hospital is neither here nor there. What Le Queux should have found out was that Pedachenko worked as a barber-surgeon for a hairdresser named Delhaye in Westmoreland Road, Walworth in 1888.'

Acting on this clue, McCormick proved that a barber of that name *had* been listed at Walworth in the London Post Office Directory of 1889. He goes even further, quoting the astonishing discovery that four of the Ripper's victims had used the same infirmary in Walworth. And further still, that Pedachenko worked in this same infirmary as an assistant. This vital information was told to Dr Dutton by Dr John Frederick Williams, who was attached to the St Saviour's Infirmary in Walworth in 1888.

To simplify the evidence (though this is difficult): Pedachenko worked as an unpaid assistant in the Walworth clinic which was used by four of the Ripper victims. It is assumed that he knew them personally, which explains why the women accompanied him so readily. At the same time, Pedachenko is named definitely as the Ripper in a document written by Rasputin. Pedachenko was sent to England by the Tsarist Secret Service to discredit the English police, and also discredit the anarchists in the East End of London by directing blame towards them.

McCormick produces another witness in support of the Russian statement, quoted by Le Queux. He refers to a conversation with a Prince Belloselski who told him that Rasputın must have dictated his statement as he was not fluent in French. He gave another translation and even more constructively produced a copy dated January 1909 of the *Ochrana Gazette*, confidential bulletin of the Tsarist secret police, revealing that Pedachenko's real name was Konovalov. This journal, issued twice a month to the various chiefs of the Ochrana, had been given to the Prince by the head of the Moscow Secret Police:

'Konovalov, Vasilly, alias Pedachenko, Alexey, alias Luiskovo, Andrey, formerly of Tver, is now officially declared to be dead. Any files or information concerning him from district sections should be sent to the Moscow Central District of Ochrana. Such information, photographs, or identification details as may still exist might refer to Konovalov, Pedachenko or Luiskovo either individually or collectively. If documents held by you do not contain these names, they should also be examined for any information concerning a man, answering to the description of the above, who was wanted for the murder of a woman in Paris in 1886, of the murder of five women in the East Quarter of London in 1888 and again of the murder of a woman in Petrograd in 1891.

'Konovalov's description is as follows: Born 1857 at Torshok, Tver. Height medium. Eyes, dark blue. Profession, junior surgeon. General description: usually wore black moustache, curled and waxed at ends. Heavy black eyebrows. Broad-shouldered but slight build. Known to disguise himself as a woman on occasions and was arrested when in woman's clothes in Petrograd before his detention in the asylum where he died.'

McCormick notices that 'the description of Konovalov tallies not only with that of the labourer, Hutchinson, but with some other descriptions of men seen with Ripper victims shortly before they met their death'. Also, that Pedachenko was known to disguise himself as a woman, which fitted the theory of Sir

Arthur Conan Doyle that 'Jack the Ripper disguised himself as a woman in order to escape from the scene of his crimes'. McCormick suggests that Pedachenko did so after the murder of Kelly, using the hot water from the kettle to shave off his moustache, and left wearing the woman's clothes he had carried in his parcel wrapped in American-cloth. Dr Dutton confirmed that Pedachenko was slightly effeminate and also ambidextrous, which fitted in conveniently. McCormick also quotes such experts as Major Griffith's who included a mad East-European doctor among his suspects.

So, finally, McCormick separates Klosowski (Chapman) and settles for Konovalov (Pedachenko) as Jack the Ripper: 'Having examined the evidence against all other suspects, one must unhesitatingly come to the conclusion that the case against Konovalov is the only one without flaws.'

The principle objection to his evidence is its sources. Ultimately, it depends on the credibility of Dr Dutton and of Le Queux. Of Dr Dutton, Colin Wilson comments that until his diaries are made public, 'it will be impossible to assess the reliability of any of his facts'. Robin Odell writes: 'It is a great pity that the doctor's work has not been made available first hand, for his views on the Ripper and other matters of criminological importance would no doubt be of great interest to several publishing houses. However, Dr Dutton seemed to have all the answers, at least to McCormick's satisfaction.'

In his revised edition, McCormick does produce 'some evidence for Dr Dutton's existence' and adds, 'I, too, fervently wish that Dr Dutton's chronicles of his crime researches had been preserved for posterity. He allowed me to take notes from them as long ago as 1923 and they covered a number of other interesting cases. By a lucky chance my notes were safely tucked away, forgotten and then rediscovered after World War II.'

As for Le Queux, Wilson describes him as a 'pathological liar' and says that Rasputin's daughter assured him 'that her father never wrote any such book, because he was not remotely interested in Russian criminals'. Odell confirms this, quoting a statement by the Tsarist police chief A. T. Vassilyev that no compromising documents were found in the search of Rasputin's apartment.

With these two sources discredited, there is little left. Some of McCormick's own deductions are far too convenient: writing of the murder of the woman in Paris (mentioned in the *Ochrana Gazette*), he attributes this to Pedachenko, and thus the Ripper, writing that: 'The dismemberment of the body was described as being unskilled, but, *except for the complete removal of the head and the dismemberment of the legs*, [my italics] the killing, especially as regards the mutilations, was similar to those perpetrated by the Ripper.' Some exception!

As for Pedachenko dressing as a woman after he killed Kelly, this seems highly improbable. Odell questions the statement that the women's clothes were carried in the parcel seen by Hutchinson, pointing out that that this was only eight inches long. Such clothes would have been flimsy indeed, for the fashion of the time. Odell suggests that if Pedachenko was going to dress as a woman he would have taken the trouble of shaving off his moustache beforehand. Indeed, how did he know there would be a fire and a kettle available; and what about the other victims? Did he shave off his curly, waxed moustache every time? Why did he take these precautions on that particular night? Such questions are interminable.

I agree with Odell's sober conclusion: 'Most of this material which was offered as evidence was third-hand or hearsay, and hardly provided conclusive grounds for believing in Dr Pedachenko at all, let alone his alleged activities in London as Jack the Ripper.' Odell makes a further excellent point in asking why Pedachenko should have restricted himself to prostitutes if he wanted to create the maximum publicity in discrediting the police? 'Surely ... his activities would have had far greater impact if he had chosen his victims from ladies, or for that matter gentlemen, of greater eminence. Then again, why did the killer, if he was thus motivated, endanger his escape by stopping to remove organs from the bodies of some of his victims? In order to shame the English police force all that he needed was to leave a trail of corpses behind him.'

Donald McCormick took part in my television programmes on the Ripper around the time that his book was being published. He refers to my discovery of Sir Melville Macnaghten's notes in his later, revised edition: 'It was quite obvious that it [his book] needed to be a completely revised and up-to-date work which paid attention to and examined in detail not only the correspondence on the subject which I have received over the past ten years, but the findings of Messrs Farson, Cullen and Odell.'

Yet it is with his use of Sir Melville Macnaghten's notes, which listed two men – Kosmanski and Ostrog – as his second and third suspects, that I feel McCormick's elaborate theory falls to pieces, almost as if he exchanges one suspect in favour of another: 'One is tempted to ask whether "Kosminski" or "Karminski" was not Klosowski. My own feeling is that 'Kosminski' is really a combination of Ostrog and one of Ostrog's associates, perhaps the double Pedachenko was said to have. Indeed the more one considers the evidence to date the more it points to Pedachenko or Konovalov as the likeliest suspect. Sir Melville's statement about Ostrog tends to confirm this, especially as Ostrog was the only one against whom he advanced sound reasons for his being suspected. Ostrog's description is so close to that of Pedachenko that they must be one and the same man. True, Sir Melville does not give a personal and physical description of Ostrog . . .' And so on.

Obviously I take this theory seriously, to examine it at such length. It is the most convincing to date, *if* the sources can be relied on. McCormick (in his 1970 revised edition) makes something of a volte face in reply to Colin Wilson's criticisms. He admits that William Le Queux 'over-dramatised his case, probably embellished it in a ridiculous fashion in a manner which helped neither his own case nor mine. But my case rests not so much on Le Queux as Dr Dutton, Prince Belloselski and other sources. Indeed it might be true to say that my case would even be strengthened if the Le Queux testimony was omitted.' This would be more acceptable if Dr Dutton was not as suspect as Le Queux.

Unless the sources can be vouched for with far greater authority McCormick's case must be discarded.

vii: *George Chapman*

One of McCormick's suspects was Severin Klosowski, later known to the police as George Chapman. Born in Poland on 14 December 1865, he came to England, probably early in 1888. This is my first objection to Chapman as a suspect: he was too young, only twenty-two years old, and too fresh to the scene to have operated with such supreme skill and confidence in a landscape that must have been totally alien to him, to say nothing of the difficulties of language.

Chapman had been a *feldscher*, as I mentioned in the last chapter, and McCormick claims that he started in a barber's shop in the basement of George Yard Buildings. This is certainly incriminating if it can be proved, for that was where Martha Turner was murdered on 7 August 1888. Later Chapman worked as an assistant in a barber's shop in Whitechapel High Street, then moved to his own shop in Tottenham and was traced by Chief Inspector Abberline, as we have seen.

On the Bank Holiday in August 1889 he 'married' a Polish woman and they lived in Cable Street until his real wife arrived from Poland; then the two women shared the house together. The legal wife left in 1890 and Chapman went to America with the other woman who returned after a quarrel. Back in the East End of London in 1893, Chapman returned to hairdressing and started his series of murders. By a strange and macabre coincidence, in view of the fact that an Annie

Chapman had been murdered by Jack the Ripper, Chapman lived with a girl called Annie Chapman, and it was then that he adopted this surname for himself. In 1895 he lived with a married woman called Spink who set him up in a hair-dressing business of his own. She played the piano while he shaved the customers, which proved popular, but she died on Christmas Day 1897, apparently from 'consumption'.

Possibly she left him some money, for Chapman took over a public house. Bessie Taylor answered an advertisement for a barmaid, 'married' him, and died from 'exhaustion from vomiting and diarrhoea'. Next he married Maud Marsh, another barmaid, and she died on 22 October 1902, but by this time the doctor was alerted and discovered arsenic in the body. Chapman was arrested for the murder of the three women by poison, and Chief Inspector Abberline made his famous comment: 'I see you caught the Ripper at last.'

One of the few shreds of evidence came from the Polish woman whom Chapman had been living with at the time of the Ripper murders. She testified that he often returned home as late as three or four in the morning and could offer no reason for these absences. Other incriminating points was a close comparison of Chapman's features to the man seen with Kelly on the night of her murder, and also that he liked to pass himself off as an American and used Americanisms in his conversation. It has been claimed this accounts for the use of Americanisms like 'Dear Boss' in the letters supposedly sent by Jack the Ripper.

But I think the converse is true, that Chapman could not have written such letters. He went to America *after* the murders and presumably his Americanisms were noticed after his return, and not before. At the time of the murders, Chapman had only been in England for a few months and it is unlikely that he could have written any letter which would have passed as being written by an Englishman, or an American for that matter. This is confirmed by a letter he sent while he was in prison fifteen years after the Ripper murders and which shows that he was still finding it difficult to write in English and had a definite, and different style of his own: 'Believe me, be careful in your life of dangers of other enemis whom are un-know to you. As you see on your own expirence in my case how I was unjustly criticised and falsly Represented.'

Yet a number of reputable people, apart from Abberline, still maintained that Chapman was the Ripper. Inspector A. F. Neil, in his book *Forty Years of Manhunting* wrote: 'We were never able to secure definite proof that Chapman was the Ripper ... In any case it is the most fitting and sensible solution to the possible identity of the murderer.' There were other sweeping deductions. In his *Trial of George Chapman,* Hargrave Adam observes that 'the first Whitechapel murder was committed shortly after Klosowski arrived in Britain and that throughout 1888 the Polish barber was living either in Whitechapel or within easy reach of the scenes of the various crimes.' With that sort of reasoning, I could make out a case against Marie Lloyd who was eighteen at the time and knew the district well.

But the overwhelming reason for disbelieving in Chapman as the Ripper is the difference in the two sets of murders. Chapman poisoned his 'wives' for his personal convenience and gain. As Colin Wilson writes in his *Encyclopaedia of Murder*, if Chapman was inspired by lust, 'he went to a great deal of trouble to sleep with three women'. It is inconceivable that he would have changed his methods in such a way, switching from the ferocity of the Ripper murders to the comparative modesty of poison. Wilson concludes, rightly, 'that there is no final evidence that he was a sadist who had to make women suffer'. As for Abberline's statement that the Ripper had been caught at last, this would have caused a sensation at the time if he had made it, or believed it to be true.

Chapman was tried in March 1903; the prosecutor was Sir Edward Carson who described him as looking 'like some evil beast. I almost expected him to leap over the dock and attack me'. The Jury was out for only eleven minutes and he was hanged on 7 April.

We must conclude that there is no factual evidence against

Chapman, quite apart from the fact that a man who destroyed so violently by the knife would have been unlikely to have turned to poison.

viii: *Dr Neil Cream*

An obvious objection to theories like the 'revengeful midwife' or the 'religious slaughterman' is the absence of any named suspect. At least George Chapman did exist. So did Dr Neil Cream who cried out on the scaffold – 'I am Jack the ——' before he was hanged – one of many to make the confession.

Cream was born in Glasgow in 1850 of well-to-do parents who emigrated to Canada when he was thirteen. He took his medical degree at McGill University but then began a life of crime. His method was poisoning by strychnine and his first or possibly second victim was an elderly epileptic called Mr Stott, in Chicago. Mr Stott's wife was Cream's mistress but everything might have passed off without suspicion if Cream hadn't written to the District Attorney advising an exhumation. Cream was a compulsive letter-writer if there ever was one, leaving a trail of incriminating clues as if, subconsciously, he wanted to be caught. Sure enough he was caught for the murder of Mr Stott, and after Mrs Stott turned State's Evidence he was sentenced to life imprisonment.

This compulsion to write letters drawing attention to his crimes is one reason for suspecting him, for the Ripper seems to have had the same urge. But it is not unusual with murderers. After his murder of Margery Gardner in a Notting Hill Gate Hotel in 1946, Neville Heath sent a letter from Worthing to the police in which he said he had lent the room to the woman, who had met an acquaintance 'with whom she was obliged to sleep' and returned to find her 'in the condition of which you are aware'. Under the name of Brooke, Heath even went to the Bournemouth police station saying he might be able to help them, though he had murdered another woman in the meantime, leaving her body in a gorge only a few miles away. A detective noticed the resemblance of Brooke to the photograph of Heath, and he was held. It is conceivable that he committed the second murder and went to the police to prove his insanity, but his first letter seems sane enough.

Cream was released from Joliet Prison in 1891, after his father had left him £5,000, and arrived in London on 1 October. On 13 October, a girl named Ellen Donworth (or Donsworth) was found in agony in Waterloo Road and died after saying that a man had given her a bottle with 'white stuff in it'. A blackmailing letter was received by the head of W. H. Smith from a Mr Bayne demanding a large sum of money for remaining silent about her murder.

In the early hours of 12 April 1892, a policeman saw a middle-aged man with a heavy moustache being let out of a Lambeth house by a young woman. An hour later he saw the girl being carried out of the house into a cab and inside he found another girl screaming in agony. One girl died in the cab, the other, Emma Shrivell, lived long enough to say that a man called 'Fred' had given them some 'long pills' after dinner. The policeman thought he recognised the moustached man in a 'Dr Neil', but when another resident of the house was shown 'Neil' he declared emphatically, 'That's not the fellow.' This put the police off the scent; it was Neil Cream who brought them back again with a letter to an eminent doctor accusing him of poisoning a girl called Matilda Clover. At Somerset House, her Death Certificate stated 'delirium tremens' as the cause, but the police noticed that the preceding name – Ellen Donworth – had died of strychnine. Clover was exhumed and strychnine found.

Not only did Cream strike up a friendship with an ex-detective and accuse a medical student, who had been a fellow-lodger, of the murders, he even went to the CID and complained that he was being followed. Among his letters was a demand for £300,000, and one to Countess Russell accusing Lord Russell of murder. Returning to America and Canada in 1892 he commissioned 500 of these cards in Quebec:

1 The corpse of Martha Turner

2 The backyard of 29 Hanbury Street, where Annie Chapman was murdered

3 The corpse of Catherine Eddowes

4 Catherine Eddowes's corpse,
suspended on the wall by pegs

Catherine Eddowes's body stitched up

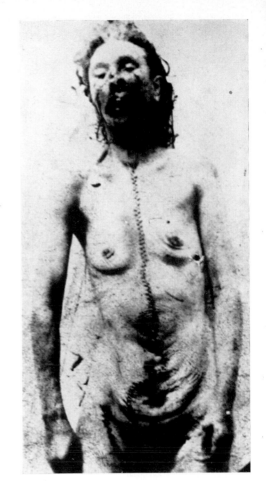

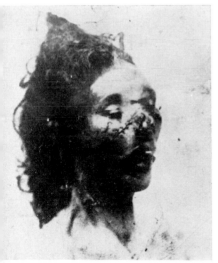

6 Catherine Eddowes

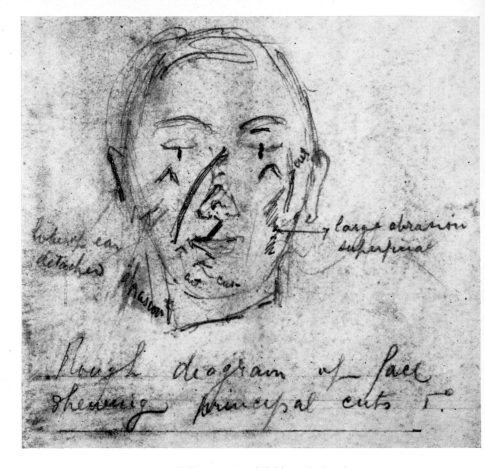

7 Police sketch of Eddowes's head

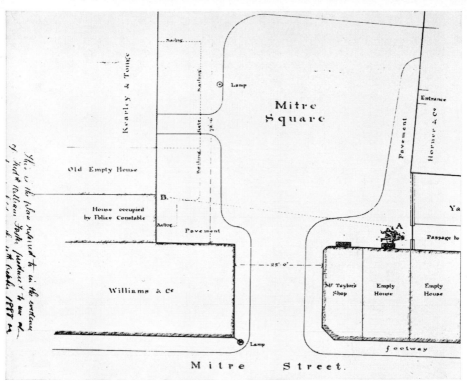

The following labels appear on the plan:

Kearley & Tonge

Railing

Lamp

Mitre
Square

Entrance

Horner & Co

Pavement

Old Empty House

B.

House occupied
by Police Constable

Pavement

A

Ya...

Passage to

25' 0"

Williams & Co

Mr Taylor's
Shop

Empty
House

Empty
House

Lamp

footway

Mitre Street.

8 Plan of Mitre Square: 'A' marks the body of Eddowes

9 Sketch of Mitre Square, looking at A from B (see plan)

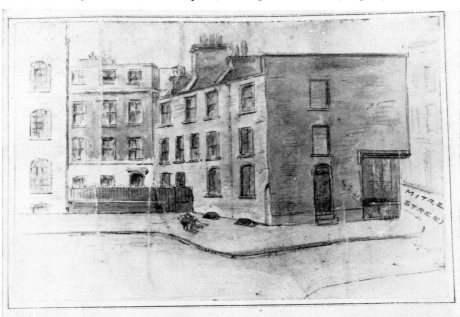

Sketch taken from point B. on plan looking towards A.

10 Miller's Court, where Mary Kelly was murdered

11 (*opposite*) The *Penny Illustrated Paper* of 17 November 1888, showing Miller's Court, with the broken window-pane wrongly marked

No. 1433.—Vol. 55
November 17, 1888

THE · PENNY
ILLUSTRATED · PAPER
AND + ILLUSTRATED TIMES

REGISTERED AT THE GENERAL POST-OFFICE AS A NEWSPAPER.

London : Printed and Published at the Office, 10, Milford-lane, Strand, in the Parish of St. Clement Danes, in the County of Middlesex, by Thomas Fox, 10, Milford-lane, Strand, aforesaid.

MILLER'S COURT

ENTRANCE TO MILLERS COURT
IN DORSET STREET

IT WAS THROUGH THE BROKEN PANES
OF THIS WINDOW THAT THE BODY
OF THE MURDERED WOMAN WAS FIRST SEEN

THE MILLER-COURT MURDER, WHITECHAPEL: SITE OF MARY KELLY'S LODGINGS.

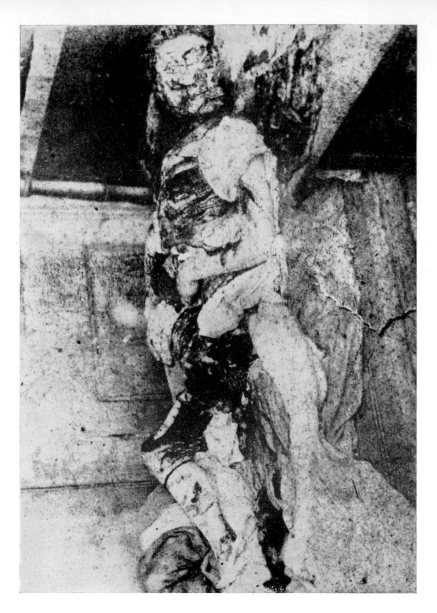

12 The corpse of Mary Kelly. This is the most extraordinary of the previously unpublished police photographs. Of it Sir Melville Macnaghten wrote, 'A photograph was taken at the time . . . without seeing which it is impossible to grasp the extent of the awful mutilation'

From hell

Mr Lusk

Sor I send you half the
Kidne I took from one women
prasarved it for you tother piece I
fried and ate it was very nise I
may send you the bloody knif that
took it out if you only wate a whil
longer

signed Catch me when
you can
Mishter Lusk —

13 The letter 'from Hell'

14 A knife used in post-mortems, now in the possession of PC
Donald Rumblelow. There is some evidence that the police
suspected that this was one of the knives that the Ripper used

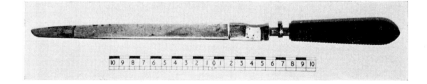

15 The Duke of Clarence

16 M. J. Druitt

17 Druitt's grave

Ellen Donsworth's Death
> To the guests of the Metropole Hotel:
> Ladies and Gentlemen,
> I hereby notify you that the person who poisoned Ellen
> Donworth on the 13th last October is today in the employ
> of the Metropole Hotel and that your lives are in danger
> as long as you remain in this Hotel.
> Yours Respectfully, W. H. Murray

In spite of such blazing self-advertisement, the police had such difficulty in obtaining actual proof that his arrest was finally for extracting money by threats. His undoing came with his last target, a prostitute called Loo Harvey whom he picked up in the Alhambra Music Hall and who had the good sense to pretend to swallow the pills after spending the night with him in a Soho hotel. She threw them over the embankment and Cream gave her five shillings to go to the Oxford Music Hall promising to see her outside at eleven. He never turned up, assuming she was dead. Dramatically, she was produced in court and identified him.

Sir Melville Macnaghten said, 'The gratification of a mad lust of cruelty was the one object of his murders,' and that 'the nearest approach we have had to him since his execution was George Chapman'. But in June 1972, the British public was shocked by the revelation of another man equally obsessed by the agony of the people he had poisoned – Graham Frederick Young.

I heard also from the son of one of the gaolers who looked after Cream before he was hanged on 15 November 1892, 'bringing him meals, etc. Cream declared several times to my father that he was Jack the Ripper.'

I don't doubt this last statement; it would have been typical of Cream's exhibitionism. Unfortunately, for such dramatic confessions Dr Cream was in Joliet Prison in America at the time of the murders.

ix: *The Social Reformer*

Another theory presents the Ripper as a public benefactor. The glare of publicity caused by the murders made people outside the East End aware of the conditions which flourished there. *The Lancet* commented in an editorial: 'It is worthy of note that the crimes have been committed in precisely the same district where, as sanitary reformers, we have often demanded the intervention of the authorities.'

Was it by accident that the Ripper chose this small area for the scene of his crimes? Was there the possibility, 'Too horrible to contemplate,' as the *Star* suggested, 'that we have a social experimentalist abroad determined to make the classes see and feel how the masses live'? Or was he 'an earnest religionist' as a writer suggested to *The Times*, 'with a delusion that he has a mission from above to extirpate vice by assassination. And he has selected his victims from a class which contributes pretty largely to the factorship of immorality and sin. I have known men and women actuated by the best and purest motives who have been dominated by an insane passion of this kind, and who honestly believed that by its indulgence they would be doing good service.'

No 'Reformer' or 'Religionist' could have chosen a better district. More real even than the tangible dangers of dirt, was the prevalence of disease, hunger, poverty and thus the consequent, inevitable prostitution. Sixty brothels were recognised officially in Whitechapel and it was claimed that two hundred lodging houses were brothels in all but name. The women were so indifferent to their fate that they joked 'I'm next for Jack', which might explain their lack of elementary caution in going with a strange man into the danger of a dark alley or backyard.

With the exposure of such conditions, people demanded that something should be done. There was a surge of sympathy from one class to another. 'Who is my neighbour?' asked *The Times*, and gave the answer: 'Unhappily for all of us, the Whitechapel murderers and their victims are neighbours of every Londoner.'

The Times published a series of letters: such as that from the Vicar of St Jude's in Whitechapel: 'The Whitechapel horrors will not be in vain if "at last" the public conscience awakes to consider the life which these horrors reveal.' *The Times* agreed: 'London at large is responsible for Whitechapel and its dens of crime. If the luxury and wealth of the west cannot find some means of mitigating the squalour and crime of the east, we shall have to abate our faith in the resources of civilisation.' Throughout the murders, *The Times* showed great humanity: 'We seem to have listlessly acquiesced in the existence of these kitchen-middens of humanity; to have treated them as though society must keep a receptacle for the collection of its waste material. We have long ago learned that neglected organic refuse breeds pestilence. Can we doubt that neglected human refuse as inevitably breeds crime, that crime reproduces itself like germs in an infected atmosphere, and becomes at each successive cultivation more deadly, more bestial, and more absolutely unrestrained?'

A still more violent blast came from a thirty-two year old dramatic critic, Bernard Shaw, in the columns of the *Star*. On 24 September, that newspaper printed his letter under the heading 'Blood Money to Whitechapel'. Referring to money raised during the dock strike two years earlier, Shaw wrote: 'The riots of 1886 brought in £78,000 and a People's Palace. It remains to be seen how much these murders may prove to be worth to the East End . . . Indeed, if the habits of duchesses only admitted of their being decoyed into Whitechapel backyards, a single experiment in slaughterhouse anatomy on an aristocratic victim might fetch in a round half million and save the necessity of sacrificing four women of the people. Such is the stark-naked reality of these abominable bastard Utopias of genteel charity, in which the poor are first robbed, and then pauperised by way of compensation, in order that the rich man may combine the luxury of the protected thief with the unctuous self-satisfaction of the pious philanthropist.'

Even Queen Victoria entered the controversy, rebuking the Home Secretary: 'The Queen fears that the detective department is not so efficient as it might be.' As this had little effect she sent a stronger telegram to the Prime Minister after the murder of Mary Kelly: 'This new most ghastly murder shows the absolute necessity for some decided action. All these courts must be lit, and our detectives improved.'

Undoubtedly, by drawing such attention in such a sensational way, the Ripper did stimulate reforms. The *Survey of London* (Vol. XXVII) acknowledged that, 'The Whitechapel murders undoubtedly gave a further impetus towards the rebuilding of the Flower and Dean Street Area.' Mrs Henrietta Barnett, wife of the Vicar of St Jude's who had written earlier to *The Times*, went so far as to claim: 'Verily it was the crucifixion of these poor lost souls which saved the district.' This was echoed by the Socialist paper *Commonweal*: 'a fiend-murderer may become a more effective reformer than all the honest propagandists in the world.' So the appeal of this theory lies in the knowledge that the Ripper did not kill in vain, and more important, that the pathetic victims did not die in vain.

The *Daily Telegraph* wrote the final word on Annie Chapman. It could serve as her epitaph: 'She has effected more by her death than many long speeches in Parliament and countless columns of letters to the newspapers could have brought about. She has forced innumerable people who never gave a serious thought before to the subject to realise how it is and where it is that our vast floating population – the waifs and strays of our thoroughfares – live and sleep at night and what sort of accommodation our rich and enlightened capital provides for them, after so many acts of Parliament passed to improve the dwellings of the poor, and so many millions spent by our Board of Works, our vestries ... "Dark Annie" will effect in one way what fifty Secretaries of State could never accomplish.'

But to say that the Ripper achieved reforms is not to say that he was motivated by a need to reform: an interesting idea with no evidence.

x: *Other suspects*

Punch parodied the possibilities that confronted the police in 'A Detective's Diary a la Mode':

Monday – Papers full of the latest tragedy. One of them suggested that the assassin was a man who wore a blue coat. Arrested three blue-coat wearers on suspicion.
Tuesday – The blue-coats proved innocent. Released. Evening journal threw out a hint that deed might have been perpetrated by a soldier. Found a small drummer-boy drunk and incapable. Conveyed him to the Station-house.
Wednesday – Drummer-boy released. Letter of anonymous correspondent to daily journal declaring that the outrage could only have been committed by a sailor. Decoyed petty officer of Penny Steamboat on shore, and suddenly arrested him.
Thursday – Petty Officer allowed to go. Hint thrown out in the correspondence columns that the crime might be traceable to a lunatic. Noticed an old gentleman purchasing a copy of *Maiwas' Revenge*. Seized him.
Friday – Lunatic despatched to an asylum. Anonymous letter received, denouncing local clergyman as the criminal. Took the reverend gentleman into custody.
Saturday – Eminent ecclesiastic set at liberty with an apology. Ascertain in a periodical that it is thought just possible that the Police may have committed the crime themselves. At the call of duty, finished the week by arresting myself!

Hunting the Ripper became a national game, in which Queen Victoria took part. 'Have the cattleboats and passenger boats been examined?' she asked her Home Secretary. 'Has any investigation been made as to the number of single men occupying rooms to themselves? The murderer's clothes must be saturated with blood?' A customs officer called Larkin, did 'prove' that the Ripper, or rather the Rippers, were two

Portuguese seamen off two cattle-boats. He worked out an elaborate chart showing that these boats had docked in London at the times of the murders. This strikes me as an example of wishful-reasoning. Taken further, it could apply to the entire population of the East End who never left the district at all. It has as much logic as the theory that Chapman was the Ripper because he had just arrived there, and left again when the murders stopped.

By arranging the facts in such a manner, it is possible to suggest that Queen Victoria herself was the Ripper – as proposed, lightly, by Oscar Tapper in *Jack the Knife* – 'the old lady herself masquerading as a mid-wife intent on revenge against a whore who crossed her beloved Albert'. In all seriousness, her own grandson has been accused, along with an extraordinary collection of types including the poet Swinburne.

The theorising and suspect-hunting perists.

In February 1972, *City* the magazine of the City of London Police, ran a story across the front page: 'Jack the Ripper – The Mystery Solved?' B. E. Reilly recalled the story of a policeman named Spicer who was patrolling his beat at Spitalfields, close to Mitre Square, on the night of the double murder. Spicer noticed 'an odd couple sitting on a brick dustbin at the end of an alleyway. One of them was a smartly dressed man, and the other a local prostitute named Rosy.'

Spicer took them into custody, but at the police station the man identified himself as a Brixton doctor and was allowed to leave without his Gladstone bag being searched. Far from congratulating him, the inspectors dismissed Spicer's suspicion and in due course he was transferred to another beat and soon left the police force altogether.

B. E. Reilly claimed that 'if his suspect was not an eccentric 'do gooder' he might well have been the murderer', and examined the Brixton doctors practising at the time. For a number of reasons a Dr Merchant who died in December 1888 seemed to be his man. Merchant was born in Poona where his father was an NCO during the Indian Mutiny, and though such a precis is unfair to him, Reilly comes to this conclusion: 'Is it not conceivable that, knowing himself to be gravely ill, the "Brixton doctor" ran amok, and dealt with the social outcasts of Victorian London as his father's regiment had treated the military outlaws in the Mutiny which left a searing impact on his young mind? Merchant, also, thought himself cleverer than the average run of doctors, as is evident from the tenor of his published letters, and may have sought a frantic outlet for his skill in these murders, characterised as they were by expert mutilations.'

Yes, it is 'conceivable'. But the theory received a nasty blow on the head in the next issue of *City* when I. M. Bartlett pointed out an addition in the policeman's own account of the story (published in the *Daily Express* in 1931): 'I left the force five months after the suspect had been released. Yet I saw the man several times after this at Liverpool Street Station accosting women. I would remark "Hello Jack! Still after them?" He would immediately bolt.' But at this time Dr Merchant was dead.

We have probably not seen the last 'suspect'; but the objection to all these theories is the lack of any concrete evidence. I am able to say with confidence that this is what I can provide, through the private notes of Sir Melville Macnaghten.

Three: The Answer

i: *The Macnaghten Papers*

My interest in the Ripper was inspired by Colin Wilson. In August 1956, after the publication of *The Outsider*, he was the first person I interviewed on television (for 'This Week'). Colin had conceived a novel based on the Ripper – 'a man on the point of insanity' – which was subsequently published as *Ritual in the Dark,* an extraordinary insight into the mentality of such a murderer and a book that has not yet been adequately recognised. As always, Colin shared his enthusiasm of the subject and told me where to look for the remaining sites of the murders. By the time I moved to the East End, in 1958, I was myself a Ripper addict. My new home was a thin house above a barge-builder's yard on the bend of the river at Limehouse. From my balcony I could see a plain brick wall a few yards to my left beside an inlet that led once to 'Dick Shoar' stairs, which is known now as 'Duke Shore' and is boarded up. This wall marks the position of the Two Brewers where the soldier was drinking before he met Martha Turner on the night she was murdered. The Two Brewers was just one of the many riverside pubs that were scattered along the Thames at that time. I discovered that my own home had been called the Waterman's Arms and I used this name when I took over a pub of my own on the Isle of Dogs.

Realising I had entered the country of Jack the Ripper, it seemed natural to include him in my television series called 'Farson's Guide to the British'. I received a deluge of replies when I made my appeal for information. Some were humorous, like the letter from two children who claimed the Ripper was their own Grannie still alive and kicking, if not actually stabbing. Some were hopelessly confused over dates. But all revealed the preoccupation with the Ripper at the time.

My dossier swelled as the letters poured in. There were several curious common factors: a grand house in Mayfair, Curzon Street, or Grosvenor Square; relatives in Bournemouth; and evidence in Australia. One letter is typical though I received it two years later. It came from a seventy-seven-year-old man who had been born in London, but now lived at Melbourne: 'When I was a nipper about 1889 I was playing in the streets about 9 p.m. when my mother called, "Come in Georgie or JTR will get you." That night a man patted me on the head and said, "Don't worry Georgie. You would be the last person JTR would touch'. [This man was his own father.] I could not remember the incident but it was brought to my mind many years later. My father was a terrible drunkard and night after night he would come home and kick my mother and us kids about something cruelly. About the year 1902 I was taught boxing and after feeling proficient to hold my own I threatened my father that if he laid a hand on my mother or brothers I would thrash him. He never did after that, but we lived in the same house and never spoke to each other. Later, I emigrated to Australia. I was booked to depart with three days' notice and my mother asked me to say goodbye to my father. It was then he told his foul history and why he did those terrible murders, and advised me to change my name because he would confess before he died. Once settled in Melbourne I assumed another name. However my father died in 1912 and I was watching the papers carefully expecting a sensational announcement.'

When there was no mention of a confession after twelve months he reverted to his real name. 'Now to explain the cause of it all. He was born 1850 and married 1876 and his greatest wish was his first-born to be a girl, which came to pass. She turned out to be an imbecile. This made my father take to drink more heavily, and in the following years all boys arrived. During the confession of those awful murders, he explained he did know what he was doing but his ambition was to get drunk and an urge to kill every prostitute that accosted him.'

Apparently, after killing one woman he drove across London Bridge and then across Waterloo Bridge to get to Covent Garden where he delivered manure, which seems a long way round. He wore two pairs of trousers and removed the outer ones which were saturated with blood, carried them under his armpit and later stowed them under some of the manure. The van stopped at the Elephant and Castle where they usually had sausage and mash. 'Jack had already told his mate that he did not want anything and was cold and would bury himself in the manure – "Don't disturb me".' While he was hidden there, he heard a policeman asking questions about the Ripper and 'was scared to death'.

G.W.B., as he signed himself, had kept this secret to himself. When he hinted to his daughter that he was related to the Ripper, 'she laughed it off saying, "You are trying to be dramatic".' More recently – for this was sent in 1961 – he had confided in a close lady friend 'and strange to say she lived in the Dandenong Ranges and it was reported that you hoped to make a discovery there' (which I shall mention in detail later). This had made him 'rather worried'. He concluded, 'Well sir, you can see, owing to my descendants I cannot disclose my name but I can assure you if I do it will be sent to you and you only. Yours G.W.B.'

I quote his letter at length, not because I regard it as unique evidence but because so many similar letters 'disappeared' with my dossier, as I shall explain. What is one to make of it? There are plenty of details, including some concerning his family in Australia which are irrelevant in this context. Yet, to me, it does not read like a work of total imagination. Nor does there seem any great wish for notoriety. It is only possible to guess, but I suspect that this and other 'confessions' are sincere, to the extent that the writer has come to believe his fantasy which may well have been based on some genuine scrap of truth in the past. At the same time, they are a distraction, and this may explain why I failed to give proper attention to an earlier letter filed in my dossier which also referred to Australia. This came from a Mr Knowles and concerned a document he had seen there called 'The East End Murderer – I knew him' by a Lionel Druitt or Drewett. The vital importance of this became clear later, and will explain why I was hoping to make a 'discovery' in the Dandenong Ranges.

In 1959, my research into the Ripper was so widespread that at one point I had two researchers working for me full-time and travelled miles myself to check on various clues. But it was by chance, as so often, that I stumbled on Macnaghten's notes, through the kindness of his daughter, Lady Aberconway.

Sir Melville Macnaghten joined Scotland Yard as assistant chief constable in 1889, when the need to establish the Ripper's identity was paramount. He became head of the CID at the Yard in 1903, when the hysteria had calmed down and judgements could be more objective. Few men could have spoken with such responsibility on behalf of the police. According to Macnaghten, all the theories I have listed can be disbelieved: 'No one ever saw the Whitechapel murderer (unless possibly it was the City PC who was on a beat near Mitre Square) and no proof could in any way ever be brought against anyone, although very many homicidal maniacs were at one time, or another suspected. I enumerate the cases of three men against whom the police held very reasonable suspicion. Personally, and after much careful and deliberate consideration, I am inclined to exonerate two of them.'

Michael Ostrog, a mad Russian doctor and convict, and unquestionably a homicidal maniac. This man was said to have been habitually cruel to women, and for a long time was known to have carried about with him surgical knives and other instruments; his antecedents were of the very worst and his whereabouts at the time of the Whitechapel murders could never be satisfactorily accounted for. He is still alive.

Kosmanski, a Polish Jew, who lived in the very heart of the district where the murders were committed. He had become insane owing to many years indulgence in solitary vices. He had a great hatred of women with strong homicidal tendencies. He was (and I believe still is) detained in a lunatic asylum about March 1889. The man in appearance strongly resembled the individual seen by the City PC near Mitre Square.

These are the men referred to, and joined together, by Donald McCormick. Confusingly, but plausibly, he uses his information to suggest that Kosmanski was Klosowski (Chapman) who might even have been the same man as Ostrog, and that Ostrog was Pedachenko, or Konovalov. But the actual evidence is slight to the point of non-existence, and they were exonerated by Macnaghten.

What then, is the case against the third suspect? Sir Melville wrote: 'But I have always held strong opinions regarding him and the more I think the matter over, the stronger do these opinions become. The *truth*, however, will never be known, and did indeed, at one time lie at the bottom of the Thames, if my conjections be correct.'

Mr M. J. Druitt, a doctor of about forty-one years of age and of fairly good family, who disappeared at the time of the Miller's Court murder, and whose body was found floating in the Thames on 3 December, i.e. seven weeks after the said murder. The body was said to have been in the water for a month, or more – on it was found a season ticket between Blackheath and London. From private information I have little doubt but that his own family suspected this man of being the Whitechapel murderer; it was alleged that he was sexually insane.

Here for the first time was the name of the police suspect. Now it was necessary to prove that Macnaghten was right. As a matter of fact he was wrong, as we soon discovered, on two points.

For an awful week it seemed there was no such person as M. J. Druitt, that Macnaghten must have been wrong altogether. No doctor could be traced of that name. No such body had been found in the Thames that month. My researcher Jeri

Matos searched at Somerset House endlessly for a death certificate for a Druitt, Drewett or Drewitt for the period in question, but with no result. Nor was there any such birth between 1845 and 50. It seemed that our suspect had neither been born nor died.

Then, in October 1959, Jeri Matos made a break-through. She traced two physicians with the name of Druitt, Robert who practised in London, and William in Dorset. Though Robert had died in 1883 and William in 1885, before the murders, we were on the trail at last. The next discovery was of a Dr Lionel Druitt, listed in the Medical Register until 1887 when his address was given as Australia. Jeri Matos soon found that Robert Druitt was Lionel's father. I returned to Somerset House to check on M. J. Druitt's suicide again. This time I met with success. Macnaghten had been mistaken in two vital details, Montague John Druitt was thirty-one and not forty-one, which is why we could not trace his birth; and though his body was found in the Thames on 31 December it was not registered until the following year, on 2 January, which is why we had not been able to trace his death; and which is why so many people before me were unable to find any record of the body that had been taken from the Thames in December, so often referred to though never named. The other mistake in Macnaghten's notes was the description of Druitt as a doctor; in fact he was a barrister.

The pieces of evidence now fell into place. William Druitt was Montague's father; Robert his uncle; Lionel his cousin. All were doctors. The Death Certificate confirmed: 'Found dead drowned by his own act whilst of unsound mind.'

Gradually a picture of Druitt began to emerge. He had been born on 15 August 1857 at West Street, Wimborne in Dorset. No birth-place could have been more tranquil than the quiet backwater of Wimborne Minster. It could be said that Druitt's background was excessively respectable. His father William was one of Wimborne's most respected men: a distinguished surgeon, a Justice of the Peace, a governor of the ancient grammar school, member of the Church Governing

Body – 'a strong Churchman and a Conservative' as the Wimborne *Guardian* described him. Montague's mother was ten years younger than his father, Anne Harvey, and also came from Dorset. He was the second son of seven children and was brought up in Westfield, one of the largest houses in the town.

It's fair to say that he was a talented boy. He went to Winchester College, thirty-five miles away, in January 1870. In September, having won a scholarship, he entered the scholars' house, 'College'. Druitt proved a successful all-rounder apart from his one appearance for the Shakespeare Society as Sir Toby Belch. His performance must have been abysmal unless he had an enemy in the critic of the *Wykehamist*, who commented: 'But of the inadequacy of Druitt as Sir Toby, what are we to say? It can be better imagined than described.'

Academically his progress was rapid. He reached the Senior Division after only three years. He came second in an English Literature prize in 1876 and was the secretary of the College Debating Society. His subjects ranged from the French Republic, which he defended, to Bismarck's influence which he attacked as 'morally and socially a curse to the world'. In his last speech he defended the present generation: 'The old theory of government was "man is made for States". Is it not a vast improvement that States should be made for man, as they are now?'

Athletically, he was a competent though not an outstanding player of Winchester Football, but he won the School Fives singles competition and played for the school cricket XI at Lords in 1876. He appears in the cricket team photograph of that year, and also in several college groups during the seventies. In his final year Druitt became Prefect of Chapel. In 1875 he sat for the Oxford and Cambridge exams and was one of the nineteen Wykehamists to be successful. In 1876 he was awarded a Winchester Scholarship to New College, Oxford.

He did moderately well at Oxford. He took a Second Class honours degree in Classical Moderations, but two years after that he only managed a Third in Greats. He left with his BA

E   113

in 1880. He had been elected Steward of the Junior Common Room which indicates his popularity with his fellow undergraduates.

It was after Winchester and Oxford that his life seems to have gone into a decline. Druitt was now twenty-three years old and decided to enter the law – an ambition that might have been encouraged by his success in the College Debating Society at Winchester. He applied for admittance to the Inner Temple and was admitted on 17 May 1882. On the 12 August, his father signed a Codicil to his long and elaborate Will saying that he had given his son a legacy of £500 to be paid after the death of his wife and after Montague's twenty-fourth birthday: 'And whereas my said son has now attained that age and has requested to make him certain advances while qualifying himself for the profession of a Barrister, Now I hereby declare that all sums of money so advanced by me during my lifetime to my said son shall be considered as part payment of the said legacy of five hundred pounds and shall be deducted therefrom.' He went on to authorise his Executor to make a further advance to Montague during the lifetime of his wife, provided that this did not exceed half of what was left. Montague was probably borrowing money for the formalities of the three years of reading for the Bar, such as the seventy-two dinners to be taken in Hall, accompanied by quantities of wine. Druitt took his finals and was called to the Bar, before the benches of the Inns of Court, on 30 March 1885. His father died of a heart attack a few months later, in September, leaving an Estate worth £16,579.

Montague did not benefit further from the will which favoured the three daughters who received £6,000 each provided they did not marry before they were twenty-one. A Dorsetshire farm, at Child Okeford, went to the eldest son who was called William after his father. The rest went to the widow.

Montague Druitt rented chambers at 9 King's Bench Walk and joined the Western Circuit and Winchester Sessions, and waited. It seems that he waited in vain. Even though this was a lean time for the legal profession it is odd that no record exists of Druitt having ever accepted a brief of any kind, especially as his brother was a solicitor on the same circuit.

In 1888, he was teaching as an assistant at the private school run by George Valentine at 9 Eliot Place in Blackheath. Once the school had been of some distinction: Benjamin Disraeli had been educated there. But by 1888 it was a 'cramming shop'. Forty-two boys as boarders, three masters, a cook and six servants, were crowded into the building. Druitt still kept his chambers at King's Bench Walk.

On 10 and 11 August, a Friday and Saturday, Druitt played for the Kingston Park Cricket Club at Bournemouth – and was bowled out for a 'duck'.

He was last seen alive on 3 December 1888.

ii: *The Missing Dossier*

None of this proves that Druitt was Jack the Ripper. Sir Melville Macnaghten's testimony is impressive in itself, but at this stage in my research there was nothing to confirm it, apart from our establishing Druitt's suicide in the Thames after the last murder. But then, slowly, I realised the significance of the letter sent to me by Mr Knowles which referred to the document he had seen in Australia : 'The East End Murderer – I knew him' by Lionel Druitt or Drewett. The relevance of this became blazingly apparent – but too late. The letter had been filed in my dossier along with others waiting to be checked, but while I was finishing the programmes my dossier vanished from Television House. I have never seen it since. I heard that the dossier had been 'borrowed' one lunchtime for someone's research and had never been returned. Apparently this person had seen a newspaper cutting about the television programmes I was preparing, and talked his way into the office. Incredibly, an assistant saw no harm in lending the man my file at the time, and, to make matters worse, she was vague as to his identity.

All researchers on the Ripper borrow from one another as I have done myself – but not so irrevocably! A wealth of material was now lost to me, and this letter in particular was vital. The only clue came several years later when I read a verbatim account of one of the interviews in the programmes which were transmitted by Associated Rediffusion in two parts in November 1959. But this was the curious case of the interview that was never shown. Originally three programmes were planned, with the quoted interview in the third. It was cut when the material was condensed to fit two programmes only: in other words, it could not have been seen on television. It must have been read, presumably from the contents of my dossier. I started legal proceedings, but then I felt there was little point in continuing at that late stage.

Also, I could hardly expect to keep my discovery of Sir Melville Macnaghten's notes secret, having publicised them on television. I gave the initials only – MJD – and blacked out the name when I showed the Death Certificate, but it was easy for any serious researcher to find out the full name from Somerset House.

Donald McCormick and Colin Wilson, who took part in the programmes and knew of the discovery, have quoted the notes, and Tom Cullen in particular made use of them in *Autumn of Terror*: 'It is these notes,' he acknowledges, 'which have furnished the basis of all subsequent assertions that Jack the Ripper committed suicide.'

Cullen supported the theory of Druitt, as far as he could go. Inevitably, there were many questions he wanted answered. Referring to the proximity of the Inner Temple, he asks: 'Does this explain his miraculous escapes? ... What was a man of his education and refined family background doing in the stews of East London? ... What ... were the contents of the letter which he addressed to Mr Valentine of the Blackheath school?' He suggests that 'if it could be found, the suicide note which Montague John Druitt addressed to Mr Valentine, for example, might throw some light on the mystery.'

Donald McCormick disputes the theory altogether: 'What other evidence is there to support Sir Melville's claim to name him as chief suspect?' he asks, and also refers to the letter which Druitt left behind him but which was never produced: 'Nor is any evidence given as to the state of Druitt's mind, nor any mention whatsoever that he had ever been seen in the vicinity of the crimes.'

These are some of the questions that must be answered. After the television programmes, I had the feeling of a mystery only partly solved. There were still too many questions, like those above, for the Druitt theory to seem wholly satisfactory. At the back of my mind was the uneasy feeling that clues existed which I had not understood. The loss of my dossier was discouraging, but when I knew I might be going to Australia I had kept notes in a separate file of places and people to visit when I finally arrived, and some of these related to the Ripper. Luckily, I had included a reference to the crucial letter from Mr Knowles about the document in Australia called 'The East End Murderer – I knew him' by a Lionel Druitt, Drewett, or Drewery, and that this had been 'printed privately by a Mr Fell of Dandenong in 1890'.

The value of this letter in identifying Jack the Ripper can hardly be exaggerated. Knowles was in his eighties then; I assume he is dead now; and I have no record of the letter which disappeared with my dossier. If anyone knows of Mr Knowles, or the document, or the existence of his letter in my dossier or wherever it might be, I hope they will come forward.

The document, 'The East End Murderer – I knew him' would have little significance if it had been written by someone unknown. But if it can be proved that it was written by Montague's cousin Lionel Druitt, who was recorded in the Medical Register as being in Australia in 1887, then it is beyond coincidence – for I received the letter from Mr Knowles before I knew of Sir Melville Macnaghten or his notes. I should perhaps, have spotted the connection at once, but it was only when I was going through my Australian file some time after the programmes had been transmitted, that I realised how vital the letter from Mr Knowles had been. Unfortunately, I did not know from what part of England he had written to me, nor his first name, though I believe it was Arthur or Alfred, and I know that it began with the initial A.

To take the matter further beyond coincidence, I received additional information from a quite separate source. This was provided by an amateur criminologist, Maurice Gould of Bexleyheath, who had written to me most helpfully during my research and had sent me a manuscript in which he claimed that Jack the Ripper was a 'cleric'. This was the 'invisible man' theory, like the postman in the detective story by G. K. Chesterton who is such a familiar figure that he goes unnoticed. His manuscript was also in the dossier, though he had kept an uncorrected draft, but several of his letters were in my Australia file, enabling me to contact him again.

Maurice Gould had been in Australia from 1925 to 1932 when he met two people who claimed they knew the identity of Jack the Ripper. This information came from papers belonging to a Mr W. G. Fell, the same surname that Knowles referred to when he said the 'East End Murderer' was printed privately by a Mr Fell of Dandenong. Today, Gould admits that details are blurred at such a distance, but he remembers that one of the two men was a free-lance journalist called Edward MacNamara who 'knew this Mr Fell of Dandenong who died in 1935' and said that Fell housed a man called Druitt who left him papers proving the Ripper's identity: 'These he would not part with unless he received a considerable sum, £500 I think, which I had not got in those days and so what I wrote was from memory from the scant examination I had of them.'

The other man who claimed to know the identity was called McCarritty or McGarritty, and was sixty years old when Gould met him in 1930: 'I lost track of him in a little place called, I think, Koo-Wee-Rup, near Lang Lang, where Fell, also an Englishman, at times looked after him.'

It was with this double confirmation of names, from Knowles and Gould, that I flew to Australia in 1961 to make a television series. Trying to trace the information further, I mentioned my search on television and in interviews with newspapers such as the Melbourne *Sunday Telegraph*. With Alan Dower, a special correspondent of the Melbourne *Truth*, I drove out to the Dandenong Ranges in search of evidence. Dower was moustached, laconic and rather tough; the Dandenong Ranges belied the promise of their name and were dull and dispiriting. But at least the places existed. We found Koo-Wee-Rup, though it is easy to overlook, and at Lang-Lang I saw the end in sight when I heard of a storekeeper called Fell – but when I met him he said he was no relation to the Fell who printed the document.

It was at another town nearby called Drouin that I met an elderly woman called Miss Stevens who remembered Dr Lionel Druitt. She said that he practised there in 1903 and that he had a daughter called Dorothy. I was unable to trace her then, but her existence was confirmed in May 1971 by Dr Peter Druitt, the great-grandson of Robert: 'I see from my copy of the family tree that he [Lionel] married a Susan Cunningham Murray, having emigrated to New South Wales in 1886. He had three daughters, Susan Catherine born in 1889, Isabella Susan Jane born 1891 and Dorothy Edith born 1899. I do not know whether these ladies are alive now or not. However, I can remember my father speaking with some affection of Dorothy, whom I believe he met whilst she was on a visit to this country many years ago, and in about 1950 I can remember meeting a Dr Henderson who came from Melbourne and who had married one of her daughters.'

At this time I still withheld the name of Druitt, out of deference to Lady Aberconway, which hampered my own efforts in tracing such relatives, but I did verify that Dr Lionel Druitt was in practise at Cooma, New South Wales in 1887; then in Koroit, Victoria in 1897; and later at Drouin. He died at Mentone, also in Victoria, on January 1908.

But there was no trace of the vital document – 'The East

End Murderer – I knew him'. Alan Dower summed up our search, made in the belief that a copy might still exist in Western Australia: 'Someone in Victoria can still finally solve the riddle of Jack the Ripper. British TV investigator Dan Farson and I are sure of this having travelled 250 miles through West Gippsland this week seeking documents and records that would provide the few missing clues.' Even without the document I had learnt a lot. I had established that Dr Lionel Druitt had lived in the district of Dandenong. It is inconceivable that he is not the same man referred to by Mr Knowles as the author of 'The East End Murderer – I knew him'. And if he was the author, then he must have made this claim with personal knowledge. The further references by Gould to the same names in the same area are also beyond coincidence.

The question remains – what personal knowledge could Lionel have had which made him accuse his cousin (though he may not have identified him by name)? Here I am able to produce another piece of crucial evidence. I discovered from the medical register that Dr Lionel Druitt had a surgery at the Minories in 1879. This is the first link between Druitt and the East End of London, the absence of which has been so baffling until now. Montague was about to leave Oxford at that date, but again I find the association beyond coincidence. There is every reason to believe that Montague and Lionel knew each other, two cousins brought up within twelve miles of each other – William's family at Wimborne, Robert's at Christchurch. Lionel was four years older than Montague and might well have felt it his duty to look after the boy when they were both in London. Lionel, a doctor, lived in the Minories at number 140, assisting Dr Thomas Thynne.

It is reasonable to assume that Montague might have visited Lionel there, and that this would explain his knowledge of the district. It is conceivable that he even lived there himself after Lionel had left, and that at some time Lionel had grounds for suspicion. Reminding me on certain points, Maurice Gould wrote to me on 6 April 1971: 'Again, if I recall correctly, it was yourself who hit upon the Minories and from that I made numerous enquiries, including a considerable time spent with an ex-head librarian of Poplar, who was a fervent 'Ripperphile'. From some recess in the library he produced an old, either Voters' List or a Directory, which listed an M. J. Druitt as living in the Minories. This fact, together with the information you unearthed about Druitt, made such a link that I think we took it for granted that he was the man we sought. Although this Druitt lived in the Minories he was not listed as a doctor as far as I can recall.' After receiving this letter, I tried to trace this reference to M. J. Druitt himself having lived in the Minories but with no success. Further enquiries indicate that the ex-librarian is dead.

The importance of the Minories is not simply their position in the East End. They have a particular significance in the story of the Ripper. On 29 September 1888, the Ripper wrote from Liverpool: 'Beware, I shall be at work on the 1st and 2nd inst., in Minories at twelve midnight, and I give the authorities a good chance, but there is never a policeman near when I am at work.'

As we have learnt, the writer of this was two days out, for Catherine Eddowes was murdered in the early hours of 30 September in Mitre Square. This is one minute's walk from the Minories. After the murder, another letter was sent from Liverpool: 'What fools the police are. I even give them the name of the street where I am living.'

Lionel Druitt was a member of the Royal Medical Society of Edinburgh; having taken his degree in surgery there in 1877. The following year he is listed at the same address as his father, Dr Robert Druitt in Kensington, but in 1879 he was listed for the first time at 140 Minories, London E. It is my belief that M. J. Druitt visited his cousin Lionel when he had his surgery in the Minories. Later, Lionel moved to 122 Clapham Road where he is listed as a junior partner of Dr Gillard in 1886. But I suggest that Montague Druitt kept in touch with the Minories and possibly rented a room there himself.

iii: *A 'Sexual Murderer'?*

Jack the Ripper was not unique; he is one of several such murderers.

Andreas Bichel, born around 1770, was known as the 'Bavarian Ripper'. He dissected the bodies of the girls like a butcher after raping them: 'In opening the breast I was so excited that I shuddered and would have liked to cut off a piece off a piece of the flesh to eat.' When he was arrested, a chest of women's clothes was found in his room and two dismembered bodies in the woodshed. The 'Ripper of Bozen' stabbed girls, in 1829, with a breadknife or penknife, choosing the lower part of the abdomen. He said he was suffering from a sexual impulse to the point of frenzy and could only find relief in the act of stabbing, when he experienced the same satisfaction as from a sexual act.

State Attorney Wulffen might have been describing Jack the Ripper in his case history of the murderer Schilling: 'We encountered an individual who was evidently excited by the contact of his hands with the soft warm flesh of his victims. He experienced a powerful urge to put his hands round the neck of a woman, to squeeze it, and finally to throttle the woman. The psychological path from throttling with the hands to stabbing and slashing with a knife is very short.'

I was wondering if the term 'sexual murderer' was too glib an explanation for the Ripper, when Colin Wilson lent me *Sexual Anomalies and Perversions* by Dr Magnus Hirschfeld, edited by Norman Haire. This book supplies some of the answers with such extraordinary relevance that Hirschfeld might have been writing about Jack the Ripper in particular. By Hirschfeld's definition, Jack the Ripper was the epitome of the sexual murderer.

He claims that 'Genuine sexual murders are far rarer than one might assume from newspaper reports.' By genuine, Hirschfeld means cases 'in which the murderer obtains sexual satisfaction by murdering or fatally injuring another person'.

He describes this in greater detail in his book *Sexual Pathology*: 'Wulffen in his *Sexual Criminal* defines sexual murder as a murder whose motives lies in a degenerated sexual impulse. It would be more accurate to say, 'a murder in which the murderer's sexual tension is released through the infliction of physical injury or death'. The act is committed in a state of sexual frenzy, if not in a state of stupefaction, and must therefore be objectively characterised as manslaughter. In a crime that deserves to be described as sexual murder the nature of the injuries is of considerable importance; *the most frequent injuries* (my italics) *are mutilations or severance of the genitals, then the ripping open of the abdomen, the tearing out of the intestines . . . In the genuine cases of sexual murder the murder takes the place of the sexual act.'*

In other words, endorsing some of the case histories mentioned above, 'There is no sexual intercourse at all; it is the slashing and tearing of the victim's body, the ripping up of the abdomen, the grubbing in the intestines, the severance and removal of the genitals, the throttling of the victim, and the sucking of her blood that produces sexual pleasure.'

This gives a great insight into the Ripper's impulses, and even makes it possible to feel a sort of pity for him. Hirschfeld makes the point that: 'The sexual murderer does not know the sinister, bestial desire to kill that lies dormant within him, to come to life at the first unfortunate opportunity.' Hirschfeld suggests that the sexual murderer is hardly aware of what he is doing – that he murders in a state of sexual intoxication.

After reading Hirschfeld, I find it easier to imagine the state of mind of Jack the Ripper, a sexual murderer with feelings of sexual inadequacy which find relief in the act of murder and mutilation which is carried out compulsively in a state of sexual intoxication, almost a daze, but in which he always retains his instinct for covering his tracks with cunning calculation. In a letter Colin Wilson writes that he agrees with my original feeling that the Ripper's motive cannot be simply defined as sexual:

'If you want my picture of Jack the Ripper' (which is what

I asked him for) 'it is of a man who feels a kind of breathless joy at the idea of destruction. Prostitutes arouse it in him because they are down and out – a sort of sadism mixed with contempt. When he kills he feels momentarily like a demon from hell who has been sent to scourge them. Forbes Winslow's theory that the Ripper was a religious reformer isn't that wide of the mark the basic intuition is right: that he feels a kind of self-righteous glee in killing. And later I think there would be intense depression, the "morning after" feeling, revulsion from the bloodstained clothes, the feeling "Did I do that?" ... I suspect that Jack the Ripper was a slave to this craving for killing, like a drug addict, but still ashamed of it.'

I am sure that Wilson is right. Apart from the question of self-acknowledged responsibility, this does not conflict with the conclusions of Hirschfeld but carries them still further.

This is more than a mere psychological digression. It is essential in linking the Ripper with Montague Druitt.

iv: *A Killer's State of Mind*

We have seen that Montague Druitt's life had been in a decline more or less since he left Winchester. In 1888 things began to go badly wrong. New evidence has been discovered by an amateur criminologist called David Anderson. Unknown to me, he had been following up the various clues ever since my programmes on television, and he contacted me when he found a report on Druitt's death in the *Acton, Chiswick and Turnham Green Gazette* for January 1889. This reveals three new points: that Druitt had been dismissed from the school at Blackheath; that Druitt's mother had become insane in July, shortly *before* the murders; and that Druitt himself feared he was going insane.

Druitt's body had been found floating in the Thames **at**

Thorneycrofts, near Chiswick, soon after midday on Monday 31 December 1888. A waterman called Winslade (referred to as Winslow in another report) brought the body ashore in his boat and notified a policeman. The body, which was well-dressed and weighted with stones in the pockets, was taken to the mortuary. The inquest was held two days later on the Wednesday, at the Lamb & Tap in Chiswick, and was conducted by the coroner, Mr Diplock.

The evidence was provided by William Druitt, Montague's brother, a solicitor who lived at Bournemouth. William lied when he claimed that his brother had no other relative. Obviously this was said to protect the family – but from what? The brothers and sisters knew that Montague was dead, for he was buried in the cemetery at Wimborne, so there must have been a greater fear than that. Sir Melville Macnaghten wrote: 'From private information I have little doubt but that his own family suspected this man of being the Whitechapel murderer; it was *alleged* that he was sexually insane.' We may suppose that William, who represented the family, believed that his brother committed the murders. But, again, why? The suicide in the Thames is no evidence in itself. Yet at the very point where the evidence might seem weakest, I can see its strength. William must have suspected Montague because he had proof. Furthermore, this proof must have been conclusive; William was not searching for notoriety, on the contrary, so he would hardly have drawn attention to his suspicions without good reason. Equally, the police would not have accepted his statement without proof – numerous people were making accusations and even 'confessions' and a suicide in the Thames would have meant little to them unless something else was involved. Druitt was the last person to be suspected *unless* there was evidence. He was no obvious candidate like Ostrog who was 'known' to have carried surgical knives, or Kosmanski who had 'homicidal tendencies'. The very 'innocence' of such a man suggests he must have been guilty to be suspected in the first place.

William Druitt testified that his brother stayed with him

at Bournemouth one night towards the end of October. At the end of December he heard from a friend that Montague had not been seen at his chambers for more than a week. 'Witness then went to London to make enquiries and at Blackheath he found that the deceased had got into serious trouble at the school and had been dismissed. That was on 30 December. Witness had deceased things searched where he resided and found a paper addressed to him (produced). The Coroner read the letter which was to this effect: 'Since Friday I felt I was going to be like mother and the best thing for me was to die.'

William stated that Montague had never tried to take his life before. The policeman, PC George Moulson, said he searched the body which was fully dressed except for the hat and collar. He found four large stones in the top coat; £2 10s. od. in gold; 7s. in silver; 2s. in bronze. There were two cheques on the London & Provincial Bank, one for £50 and the other for £16; I have tried to trace these with the help of the archivist of Barclay's Bank which absorbed the London & Provincial, but with no success. It has been suggested that these cheques were drawn by Druitt to pay off a blackmailer, but it is far more likely they were drawn by George Valentine, the headmaster of the school in Blackheath, in full and final settlement after his dimissal.

There was also a first-class season pass from Blackheath to London (South Western Railway), and a second half return from Hammersmith to Charing Cross, dated 1 December. This was the day the school broke up for the Christmas holidays, and it is possible that Druitt had a reason for visiting Hammersmith, close to Chiswick where his body was found. His mother died in a private mental home in Chiswick on 15 December 1890 of 'melancholia' and 'brain disease, 21 months'. Because of this figure of twenty-one months, it has been assumed (by Cullen) that Druitt's mother 'never recovered from the shock' of his suicide, and became insane afterwards partly because of it. But William's evidence shows that his mother was already insane and possibly already in the mental home in Chiswick, which would explain his visits to this district, and his fear he was becoming like her.

Also on the body, was a silver watch with a gold chain and spade King attached; a pair of kid gloves; and a white hand-kerchief. There were no papers or letters of any kind – unless the policeman had been instructed to say this – and there were no marks on the body which was rather decomposed. A verdict of suicide was returned and Montague was buried the next afternoon at Wimborne Cemetery, where the cross still stands today: 'In Memory of Montague John Druitt, who died 4 December 1888. Aged 31.'

With the discovery of Druitt's body, the official search for Jack the Ripper came to an end. The various references to 'the body in the Thames' suggests this was not a coincidence. Many other people seem to have had the same source of information as that of Sir Melville Macnaghten. It is worth quoting some of them: Major Arthur Griffiths, Inspector of Prisons and author of *Mysteries of Police and Crime*: 'There is every reason to believe that his own friends entertained grave doubts about him. He also was a doctor in the prime of life, was believed to be insane, or on the borderline of insanity, and he disappeared immediately after the last murder, that in Miller's Court on 9 November 1888. On the last day of that year, seven weeks later, his body was found floating in the Thames and was said to have been in the water a month.' Albert Backert of the Whitechapel Vigilance Committee: 'I was given this information in confidence about March 1889. It was then suggested to me (by the police) that the Vigilance Committee and its patrols might be disbanded as the police were quite certain that the Ripper was dead . . . He was fished out of the Thames two months ago and it would only cause pain to relatives if we said any more than that;' Watkin Williams, the grandson of Sir Charles Warren: 'My impression is that he believed the murderer to be a sex-maniac who committed suicide after the Miller's Court murder – possibly the young doctor whose body was found in the Thames on 31 December 1888;' Sir John Moylan, Assistant Under Secretary at the

Home Office: 'The murderer, it is now certain, escaped justice by committing suicide at the end of 1888;' Sir Basil Thomson, Assistant Commissioner of the CID in 1913: 'In the belief of the police, he was a man who committed suicide in the Thames at the end of 1888.'

Sir Harold Scott, an ex-Commissioner of Police, accurately identified the suspect as a 'barrister' when he wrote about the Ripper in the *Concise Encyclopaedia of Crime and Criminals* in 1961, but many people were confused by the constant assertion that he was doctor.

Leonard Matters wrote in 1926 that he had 'searched the columns of *The Times*, the *Daily Telegraph*, the *Daily News* and the *Star*, and have failed to find any reference between 9 November 1888 and March 1889 to this sensational find in the Thames.' Of course he, and others like him, were looking in vain for a specific reference to the suicide of a doctor, but it was fair enough to ask why 'no sensational account' was to be found in the press if the police had really caught such an infamous character. Part of the answer may be that the police were genuinely reluctant to involve Druitt's family in the aftermath of such a scandal. Backert was told, 'it would only cause pain to relatives if we said any more than that', and when he persisted the police warned him that his pledge to secrecy was 'a solemn matter, that anyone who put out stories that the Ripper was still alive might be proceeded against for causing a public mischief'. It should be noted that the police were still arresting suspects in November; it was after Druitt's body was discovered in December that arrests ceased.

In fact we may agree that the police were right to have protected the family. In the same way, in the recent case of the Nude Murders, they spared the family after their suspect also committed suicide, and achieved a minimum of publicity.

Gradually, the Ripper and Montague Druitt come together. The police and other officials believed the Ripper was drowned in the Thames at the end of December; Sir Melville Macnaghten establishes that this man was Druitt. Druitt's suicide is a vital part of the pattern: 'Murderers of this sort *don't* stop,' Professor Camps has assured me, and he has written elsewhere: 'Sadistic killers of his type do not "burn out" or "retire" – hence the person involved after the perpetration of the last murder must have been out of circulation. There are only a limited number of ways in which this can happen – death, emigration, or incarceration either in a prison or mental hospital.' As for Druitt, 'This is the type of person you're looking for,' Professor Camps has told me. 'He wouldn't have stopped had he lived.'

Could not Druitt's suicide have been due to something else, unconnected with the murders? Of course it could; but there is the crucial fact that the police and his own family did not think so. I am not convinced by the alternative explanation for his suicide put forward by Donald McCormick, who quotes a mysterious figure, a London doctor whose father was at Oxford with Druitt: 'He always told me that the story about Druitt being the Ripper arose through the barrister being blackmailed by someone who threatened to denounce him as Jack the Ripper to the school where he worked. Whether this was a heartless hoax or a cruel method of extorting money from a man who was just recovering from a nervous breakdown was not clear. There was nothing seriously wrong with Druitt, but he suffered from insomnia and black-outs and these threats preyed on his mind and paved the way to a further breakdown.'

This man's father, who was also an experienced doctor, was convinced that Druitt was not the Ripper and that the gold found on his body was to pay off the blackmailer. Also that Druitt had told his mother all about it and that anyhow Druitt was definitely in Bournemouth when the first two crimes were committed. As this is unsubstantiated, it would be helpful if this 'London doctor' could be traced, which I have been unable to do. Again it is assumed that Druitt's mother became insane after the murders, which was not the case. As for the money, this is more likely to have been payment from the school, as I have suggested. And if he had been in Bournemouth at the time of the first two murders he would never have been suspected at all.

McCormick concludes: 'This seems finally to dispose of the
case that Druitt had any connection with the crimes.' This is
wonderfully topsy-turvy reasoning. If the doctor's story is
genuine, it is far more likely that Druitt was being blackmailed
at the school because he was indeed Jack the Ripper or had
given reason for such a suspicion. This is infinitely more convincing than the explanation of 'a heartless hoax'.

v: 'The Answer at Last'

We can now build up the 'case against Druitt'. As far as
physical description and personality Druitt is closer to the
Ripper than the concept of a black-bearded Russian lunatic.
(Christie was described as respectable; Marie Kendall told me
that Dr Crippen was 'an unassuming little man'; it is doubtful
if the Ripper appeared any more remarkable.) Most of the
experts agree with this theory: Colin Wilson: 'It is far more
likely that the Ripper was an upper- or middle-class
young man, with some powerful grudge against the world
or his family, than that he was a crazy Russian doctor or
barber-surgeon;' Robin Odell: 'The popular suggestion that
the Ripper was a wild-eyed frenzied maniac lurking the streets
in fulfilment of his blood-lust did less than justice to the facts.
In the first place, a man of this type would never have succeeded in gaining the quiet confidence of his intended victims.
This particular aspect of the evidence has perhaps never been
accorded its due place of importance;' Leonard Matters:
'The whole weight of reason, if not of evidence, in the mystery
is undeniably against the theory that "Jack the Ripper" was, in
the ordinary acceptance of the word, a lunatic. He was not a
madman bereft of reason, comprehension, capacity for cool
thinking and most methodical conduct . . . "'Jack the Ripper"
– disguised or otherwise – must have mingled with hundreds of
people in the East End. It is not to me extraordinary that

he did not attract marked attention. He was more sane and normal in his speech and conduct than ninety-nine per cent of those he met!'

Druitt fits all these generalisations and even the particular physical description by the commercial traveller Lawende who saw Catherine Eddowes talking to a man ten minutes before she was killed. This is the only 'eye-witness' who is worth taking seriously: 'Thirty years old, five feet nine inches in height, with a small fair moustache, dressed in something like navy serge and with a deerstalker's hat, peak fore and aft.' Druitt was thirty-one, and although it is hard to judge from the photograph just how dark or fair he was, there is the beginning of a small moustache.

There is one further piece of evidence that could be significant in linking Druitt and the Ripper. Much has been made of the suggestion that the Ripper was ambidextrous. Writing of the third police suspect in *Mysteries of Police and Crime,* the suicide in the Thames that was plainly Druitt, Major Griffiths commented: 'It would be interesting to note whether in this third case the man was left-handed or ambidextrous, both suggestions having been advanced by medical experts after viewing the victims.' Though the evidence relating to this was staring me in the face, I wrote to James Sabben-Clare, the Curator of Wiccamica at Winchester College who has been very helpful throughout; he sent me this reply: 'MJD's sporting career should give us a clue to his use of his hands. Now he was a very good player at Fives, as I told you, and actually won the School Singles title ... to be that good [the game is played with both hands, rather than a bat] he must at least have had a lot of strength in both arms and wrists.' Sabben-Clare adds that here is some, though not conclusive, evidence that Druitt bowled left-handed.

The police photographs convey an instant impression of how the murderer ripped his victims apart. In the same way, our knowledge of the extra strength in both arms conveys a further impression of the way Druitt worked, stabbing fiercely with both hands at ferocious speed. It makes one think again of the possibility that Martha Turner was a Ripper victim. The surgeon, Dr Timothy Keleene, was convinced that two weapons had been used. Quoting this evidence, McCormick asks: 'Why should the killer use two weapons? That was the poser which the police asked themselves in vain. The obvious deduction was that the murderer was ambidextrous: certainly he could deliver blows as effectively with one hand as with the other.'

The point about 'medical knowledge' also fits. Keleene, whom I have just quoted, thought that the murderer used a long-bladed knife and possibly a surgical instrument when he killed Martha Turner. He doubted the theory that the murderer was a soldier because he thought that he must have an elementary knowledge of surgery; 'Whoever it was, he knew how and where to cut.'

Even if Martha Turner was killed by someone else. The charges of 'medical knowledge' flourished after the later murders. Keleene's testimony was more considered than most. In the case of Mary Nicholls, Dr Llewellyn claimed that the mutilations were 'deftly and skilfully performed'. In the case of Annie Chapman, Dr Bagster Phillips, the Metropolitan Police Surgeon, said that if he had been removing the organs deliberately, in an autopsy, it would have taken him the better part of an hour, and that he could not have performed the mutilations himself in under a quarter of an hour. *The Times* confirmed: 'The murderer gives proof of anatomical skill.' In the case of Eddowes, Dr Brown also said that the murderer had anatomical skill; but two of the other doctors, Sequera and Saunders, disagreed.

It seems to me that there is every reason for believing that the Ripper was not a doctor. I came to this conclusion when I started my research in 1959 and visited the pathologist, Dr Keith Simpson, in an office decorated with such objects as a piece of flesh in a bottle bearing the teeth-marks of Neville Heath. Dr Simpson told me that he had never believed in the 'doctor' theory. He argued that if the Ripper had been a doctor his lust for cutting up bodies would have been satisfied by his work, or would have been so extreme that his colleagues would have noticed it. There would not have been that additional urge to turn to murder.

Though it's virtually certain that the Ripper was not a doctor, I believe he did have some basic medical or surgical knowledge. Druitt's own father, uncle and his cousin Lionel were all doctors. He was brought up in a medical atmosphere and may well have attended post-mortems. He would have had easy access to surgical instruments. One weapon which the police suspected that the Ripper used is a post-mortem knife (see illustration no. 14). The proximity of the 'surgery' might even have had a stimulating effect on Druitt, (as the butcher's shop had on the French murder Eusebius Pieydagnelle who was tried in 1871 for four murders. He was at his happiest when he was apprenticed to a butcher:' The sweetest sensation is when you feel the animal trembling under your knife. The animal's departing life creeps along the blade right up your hand.')

Some elementary knowledge was evident – the kidney, for example, is a difficult organ to find and extract in such circumstances. In other words, the Ripper was not a doctor but seems to have had some rudimentary knowledge and possibly access to surgical instruments. Montague Druitt meets such requirements.

Thirdly, the question of location fits Druitt. I am certain that the Ripper had access to some private room near the scene of the murders. A doss-house, or any communal lodging house would have been far too dangerous. A private room would explain why the murders were committed within such a small radius, and how he managed to escape.

There is exaggeration in the picture of the Ripper leaving the scene of the crime dripping with blood, clutching his little black bag with its surgical weapons. There was remarkably little blood, owing to the strangulation of his victims, and he would only have needed a knife or two and the pockets to hide them in. At the same time, he was not the man to take risks and there must have been stains of some sort. These would have been especially noticeable in the light of day after the last murder, which supports the theory that both Mary Kelly and the Ripper had stripped naked before the holocaust began. But every time, the Ripper must have hurried to his lair as rapidly as possible.

If Druitt kept in touch with the surgery in the Minories, even passing himself off as a doctor, we would have a simple explanation. The Minories is only ten or fifteen minutes walk from all the murders. Few places could have been so convenient. But even if I am wrong, Druitt could have walked back to the Temple and his chambers at 9 King's Bench Walk, after washing himself free of blood as he seems to have done after murdering Eddowes in Mitre Square. From there, the journey would have taken half an hour, or so.

The evidence of the London-Blackheath season ticket found on Druitt's body has been examined skilfully by Tom Cullen who claims that this indicates that Druitt did not live at Blackheath. He has discovered that the last train left Cannon Street at 11:40 p.m. and London Bridge at 12:25 a.m., which rules out any idea that he might have caught such a train after the murders. The first train left Cannon Street at 5:10 a.m., which would have left uncomfortable hours to kill.

Perhaps there is a clue in the statement by William Druitt at the inquest. He refers first to his brother's 'chambers' but a moment later he uses the different phrase 'where he resided'. I may be reading too much into this, but it strikes me that the second reference is to another place, and that the use of words indicates this was not the Temple where he still had an 'address'. It would be more likely to refer to another room altogether. Could this have been in the Minories, as told to Maurice Gould by the ex-librarian?

Lastly the letters need to be examined, even though the result is inconclusive. Though it is in character for the murderer to have written such boastful, exhibitionistic letters, there is the problem of deciding which communications are genuine. Because of the evidence regarding the kidneys of Catherine Eddowes, I regard the letter to Mr Lusk as the most likely (see illustration no. 13). In its exaggerated style, almost stage cockney – 'prasarved it for you, tother piece I fried' – I see an educated man pretending to be illiterate, It is unlikely that an ill-educated man would have written the word 'knif', and that this would come to him more readily as 'nife'. In the note from Glasgow, this was corrected: 'Think I'll quit using my nice sharp knife. Too good for whores. Have come here to buy a Scotch dirk. Ha! Ha! That will tickle up their ovaries.' Again, I wonder if an illiterate man would have been familiar with the word *ovaries*.

There is also a curious aspect of the famous 'Dear Boss' letter which is signed 'Jack the Ripper' or rather there is something curious about the envelope, which is usually overlooked. This is addressed to: 'Dr Openshaw Pathological Curator of the London Hospital, Whitechapel.' It is odd that an uneducated man should send a letter to the 'Pathological Curator' rather than the police or a newspaper. But with Druitt's knowledge of the medical world, this would have been natural. Then he would have disguised his style in the actual letter accordingly.

The amateur criminologist, David Anderson, has succeeded in finding specimens of Druitt's signature but according to the expert graphological opinion of P. G. Baxter these neither prove not disprove a connection with the letter sent to Mr Lusk. This is largely due to the fact that the copies are poor quality reproductions 'removed from the originals by a number of generations, and each copying process has reduced the fine detail'. Also, a signature is hardly enough to go on. Consequently, Mr Baxter was reluctant to make a comparison between Druitt's signature and the Lusk letter: 'We are dealing with a period in history,' Mr Baxter wrote to me in explanation, 'when handwriting was taught to a specific stylised pattern or copybook form; therefore much more regularity is to be observed in writing of this period than in specimens of today. It is an accepted view that in this period two different handwritings by one person was uncommon, and this for the reasons of the methods of teaching which were particularly harsh. A style was rigidly adhered to by the teacher and copied laboriously by the pupil until writing became an almost automatic habit. Modifications to the learned pattern or style were rare although not entirely unknown, development of 'personal' style was not encouraged thus much writing of this period bears a superficial resemblance.'

On the 'Ripper correspondence' in general, Mr Baxter believes that more than one person was involved. Regarding the two specimens I sent to him – copies of Druitt's signature and the letter to Lusk – he writes, 'Whilst it is not possible to state with certainty that the person now suspected is not the writer of the submitted material – the converse is equally true. There is no good evidence that the suspected person did not write the "Ripper" letters.'

An interesting comment on the Ripper's handwriting comes from the Canadian graphologist C. M. Macleod, published in the *Criminologist* in August 1968. He also refers to the letters concerning the kidneys, the one to Lusk, sent from Hell, in a large almost ornate hand, though rather stained, and the other more untidy letter sent to Major Smith: 'Old Boss you was rite it was the left kidny . .' To the layman, it does not look as if they are written by the same person, which Macleod confirms.

He describes the 'knife-edged or daggerlike strokes' in the word 'Kidne' in the Lusk letter as a 'strongly negative feature': 'When sharp angles and dagger strokes are combined with all the other negative features shown in both samples, one may be absolutely confident that the writer has strongly negative impulses towards others, and might very well give vent to them in destructive outbursts.'

Referring to the smears and muddiness in both letters, he says, 'they were probably both heavy drinkers,' and having discussed the similarities Macleod points out the differences especially in the letter 'I': 'It is a graphological axiom that this one letter word reveals more than any other sign what the writer actually thinks of himself. In sample 1, we find a high-flying capital I revealing self-confidence to the point of cockiness. In sample 2 [the letter to Smith], we find what to me is an extremely rare phenomenon: the lower case "i" written smaller than many of the lower case letters. The writer was evidently familiar with the theory of capitals, since he begins both his letter and his verse with a curiously flooded o and attempts a capital in *Jack*. The fact that he elected not to use this most important capital letter of all suggests an overweening sense of his inferiority, which may well have triggered intense *hostility toward anyone who might represent the mother he no doubt held responsible for his failure as a person.*' (My italics, for obvious reasons relating to Druitt and his fear of becoming like his mother.)

But after careful and clever analysis, Mr Macleod makes his conclusion that 'If there was only one real Jack the Ripper, I should cast my vote for the writer of sample 1 [to Lusk]. He shows tremendous drive in the vicious forward thrust of his overall writing, and great cunning in his covering-up of strokes; that is, the retracing of one stroke of a letter over another, rendering it illegible while appearing to clarify. While sample 1 appears to be written better than sample 2, it is in fact extremely difficult to decipher; whereas sample 2, except for the atrocious spelling, is fairly readable.

'I would say that this writer was capable of conceiving any atrocity, and of carrying it out in an organised way. I would say he had enough brains and control to hold down some steady job which would give him a cover for his crimes. He has imagination, as revealed in the upper-zone flourishes. Those hooks on the t-bars, among other signs, indicate tenacity to achieve a goal.'

Macleod also detects a latent homosexuality. This is not incompatible with Druitt's character and might explain the 'trouble' at school which led to his dismissal. Of course the 'hostility towards anyone who might represent the mother' in the second letter is even more compatible.

Before I sum up, I should mention that I have been in touch with Dr Peter Druitt at Christchurch near Bournemouth, the great-grandson of Dr Robert Druitt (1814–1883), a surgeon who was highly thought of in his day. Robert was Lionel's

father and Montague's uncle. I wrote to Dr Druitt in the
first place because I was anxious not to distress his family,
and received this welcome reply: 'I do assure you that the
subject causes me no distress whatever. In a macabre way it
livens up an otherwise dull, though very worthy, ancestry.' He
adds that 'the Druitt family has largely died out'.

vi: *Conclusion*

The turning point in my research came in 1959 when Christabel
Aberconway let me see the private notes of her father Sir
Melville Macnaghten who identified Montague John Druitt as
the leading police suspect. More recently, I have had support
for the theory from the two leading experts on the subject
today. Professor Francis Camps is an expert on crime in general
and has always been interested in the case of Jack the Ripper.
In May 1971 I spent an absorbing afternoon – which became
an evening – in his Barbican apartment, along with his assistant
at the London Hospital, Sam Hardy, and PC Donald
Rumbelow. Professor Camps has that irresistible combination
of a lucid brain with boyish enthusiasm. 'He's the type of
person you're looking for' he said of Druitt, 'He's the only
one who fits. I always thought the Ripper was well-educated.'
Later he was kind enough to write to me: 'I really must
congratulate you on your research. I am sure you have got the
answer at last.' Finally he was generous enough to write the
foreword to this book. I am lucky enough to have had the
additional support of Colin Wilson. He confirms that Druitt
is the most likely suspect of all.

We can recapitulate several points: William Druitt the
elder brother, believed that Montague was the Ripper; several
leading representatives of the police and Home Office made
separate statements claiming the Ripper was found in the

Thames at the end of December 1888; undeniably this man was Druitt; a link is established between Druitt and the East End with the existence of Dr Lionel Druitt's surgery in the Minories as early as 1879. The Minories was referred to in one of the 'letters from the Ripper' and lies within a few minutes walk of the various murders; reference has been made to a document written by Lionel Druitt printed privately by a Mr Fell of Dandenong in Australia in 1890. The document was called – 'The East End Murderer – I knew him'. It has been proved that his cousin, Dr Lionel Druitt did indeed practice there, and a separate source confirms the existence of Mr Fell; Montague Druitt was ambidextrous; he may well have had surgical knowledge; he feared he was going insane, like his mother; above all, his brother and the police must have been in possession of some proof to believe that Montague Druitt was the Ripper.

I gather that the official files in Scotland Yard, which are not open to the public until 1992, confirm my conclusions and have little else to add.

Finally, I have traced a photograph of Montague John Druitt, which is published here for the first time. Though this was taken when he was at Winchester, he looks surprisingly mature. Do the eyes have a slight madness, or is that only in the knowledge that we have today? Shall we ever know for certain the impulse behind those eyes, the pressure that released the murderer inside the man who terrorised London in 1888?

I believe that final pieces of evidence still exist in England or Australia such as a copy of the document 'The East End Murderer – I knew him' – which will close the file for ever. Yet now that I am at the end of my journey, I feel like postponing the arrival. To 'catch' the Ripper at last would be an achievement, but also it would spoil the legend that persists throughout the years. Perhaps the Ripper should remain a mystery.

As for Druitt, if he was the Ripper, I can sense his own terror. Though my theory stems from Sir Melville Macnaghten

I cannot agree exactly with his conclusion that 'after his awful glut [in Miller's Court] his brain gave way altogether'.

I prefer to believe that as he walked into the cold void of dawn, satiated yet empty, his brain trembled for a moment and he realised what he had done. He revealed this knowledge in papers left for his brother William, and then took his own appalled and appalling life.

INDEX